THE FREEDOM OF
GOD'S SONS

THE FREEDOM OF GOD'S SONS

Studies in Galatians

by
Homer A. Kent, Jr.

BMH BOOKS
WINONA LAKE, INDIANA

To my brother
WENDELL
companion of boyhood days
and faithful preacher
of the gospel of Christ

Acknowledgments

A book is usually the result of an author's considerable effort. Nevertheless few literary works come from one mind alone. The present little volume has drawn from the labors of many who have blazed trails in Galatians. In addition, I am specially indebted to those who are named below.

Dr. John C. Whitcomb, Jr., my colleague for twenty-five years in the teaching of God's Word at Grace Theological Seminary, read the manuscript and made valuable suggestions.

Dr. James L. Boyer, my associate in the New Testament Department, granted permission for the use of his New Testament Chronological Chart, from which an adaptation appears as Fig. 4.

Professor Robert D. Ibach, Jr., another faithful colleague, prepared the maps and charts.

Mrs. Shirley Fischbach provided her secretarial skills in the typing of the manuscript.

Finally, a special word of appreciation is due to Charles Turner of BMH Books and Cornelius Zylstra of Baker Book House for their unflagging courtesy and encouragement.

Contents

Illustrations

Picture Credits

Dr. Donald W. Burdick, Conservative Baptist Theological Seminary, Denver, Colorado.

Cambridge University Library, Cambridge, England CB3 9DR

Levant Photo and Design Service, P.O. Box 1284, Santa Cruz, California 95060.

The Metropolitan Museum of Art, New York, N.Y. 10028.

Kelsey Museum of Archaeology, The University of Michigan.

Transliteration Table

Whenever possible, Hebrew and Greek words have been transliterated according to the following form:

Greek	Hebrew Consonants	Hebrew Vocalization
a — a	א — '	— ā
ϵ — e	ב — b, b̲	— a
η — ē	ג — g, g̲	— e
o — o	ד — d, d̲	— ē
ω — ō	ה — h	— ê
ζ — z	ו — w	— i
θ — th	ז — z	— î
ξ — x	ח — ḥ	— o
υ — u	ט — ṭ	— o
ϕ — ph	י — y	— û
χ — ch	כ — k, k̲	— u
ψ — ps	ל — l	— ( )e
' — h	מ — m	
$\dot{\rho}$ — rh	נ — n	
α — āi	ס — s	
η — ēi	ע — '	
ω — ōi	פ — p, p̲	
$\gamma\gamma$ — ng	צ — ṣ	
$\gamma\kappa$ — nk	ק — q	
$\gamma\xi$ — nx	ר — r	
$\gamma\chi$ — nch	שׂ — ś	
	שׁ — š	
	ת — t, t̲	

Abbreviations

Arndt	*A Greek-English Lexicon of the New Testament,* by William F. Arndt and F. Wilbur Gingrich
ASV	American Standard Version, 1901
EGT	*The Expositor's Greek Testament*
KJV	King James Version, 1611
LXX	Septuagint (Greek translation of the OT)
NASB	New American Standard Bible, 1971
Nestle	*Novum Testamentum Graece*
NIV	New International Version, 1973
NT	New Testament
OT	Old Testament
TDNT	*Theological Dictionary of the New Testament*

Preface

Paul's Epistle to the Galatians stands with his Epistle to the Romans as influencing Christian thought and history perhaps more than any other New Testament book. It is conceivable, humanly speaking, that Christianity might have become merely another Jewish sect if the argument of Galatians had not become the prevailing view of the church. In the days of the Reformation, this epistle had great influence on Martin Luther, and his lectures on it in 1531 are still preserved. He said of it: "The Epistle to the Galatians is my epistle. To it I am as it were in wedlock. It is my Katherine."[1] Its significance is no less today, for the threat of human works as an alternative to the saving grace of God still lurks in the hearts of men and seeks to turn them from the gospel of Christ.

Although there is no scarcity of studies on Galatians, I accepted the invitation to contribute this volume in the New Testament Studies series with the conviction that every fresh look at the Word of God will bear its fruit because of the inexhaustible riches of Scripture. By the use of photographs, maps, charts, and exposition, it is hoped that the message of Galatians will come alive to the modern reader, and that he will thrill as did Paul at the realization of the freedom that belongs to the sons of God.

Homer A. Kent, Jr.

Winona Lake, Indiana

---

[1]Martin Luther, *A Commentary on St. Paul's Epistle to the Galatians*, trans. Theodore Graebner (Grand Rapids, n.d.), p. iv.

Introduction

The first theological problem of any consequence to erupt in the early church involved the relation of Gentile converts to the Mosaic Law. Could Gentiles become true Christians without observing Jewish rites? The problem was an obvious one. After all, the first Christians were Jews, and they had been faithful adherents of Mosaic traditions. They had been taught, and properly so, that trust in Jesus as Messiah and Lord was the correct Jewish response to the long-awaited redemptive program of God. Christian faith, to these early believers, was no radical departure from the hope of their fathers, but was the step that should have been taken by every Jew. Consequently, it should not be the least surprising that many early Christians would suppose that if Gentiles were to enjoy the blessing of the God of Abraham, they should also conform as fully as possible to the religious practices that Jewish Christians had always observed.

The question of obligation to the Mosaic Law on the part of Gentile Christians arose in various ways in the early church. Even though Peter had proclaimed at Pentecost that the gospel invitation included "all that are afar off, even as many as the Lord our God shall call" (Acts 2:39), it required a special revelation from God before Peter understood some of the implications of that pronouncement (Acts 10:9-16, 28, 34-35). The Jerusalem church as a whole was no more perceptive. When Peter returned from Caesarea after bringing the gospel to the Gentile Cornelius, he was challenged by some, not because he had baptized a Gentile but because he had entered into social relations that violated the usual kosher regulations of Jewish practice (Acts 11:3). To the credit of the Jerusalem church, it must be observed that the explanation by Peter was sufficiently convincing to ease the tension for a time (Acts 11:18); but the problem arose again a few years later. By that time the very possibility of Gentile salvation apart from Jewish rites was being questioned, and the crucial Jerusalem Council was held to deal with the issue (Acts 15).

What made this particular theological problem such an explosive issue was its immediate relationship to daily life. It dealt with the way people lived, for the Mosaic Law regulated the lives of its adherents in minute details. Involved were matters of religious observances, social contacts, and dietary habits, as well as a whole philosophy of life that had been developed from it by rabbinical interpreters through the centuries.

The Epistle to the Galatians is addressed to this problem. It remains as the definitive statement on the problem of legalism in contrast to the Christian faith.

Authorship

The Epistle to the Galatians claims to have been written by the apostle Paul (1:1; 5:2), and Pauline authorship is not generally doubted today. Except for a few radical Dutch critics,[1] whose views have been largely discounted by even liberal scholars,[2] there is little question of the genuineness of Galatians. It is commonly recognized as one of the four chief epistles of Paul (along with Romans and I and II Corinthians).

This almost universal recognition of the epistle as Paul's is fully supported by the testimony of early church history. There may be an allusion to the wording of Galatians in the very earliest extant Christian document, the First Epistle of Clement to the Corinthians (A.D. 96), and further allusions or indirect citations from the early second century are found in Ignatius, Polycarp, Barnabas, and Hermas.[3] By the end of the second century it was clearly used as Paul's by such as Irenaeus, Clement of Alexandria, Tertullian, and the Muratorian Canon.

Nothing in the epistle is inconsistent with Pauline teaching elsewhere. On the contrary, the careful explanations in Gala-

---

[1]For further discussion, see Herman N. Ridderbos, *The Epistle of Paul to the Churches of Galatia* (Grand Rapids, 1956), pp. 35-36.

[2]For example, J. Knox writes: "There can be no serious question about the authorship of this letter" ("Letter to the Galatians," *Interpreter's Dictionary of the Bible*, ed. George H. Buttrick, New York, 1962), E-J, 338.

[3]A detailed listing of early references is given in the old but still valuable work by J. B. Lightfoot, *The Epistle of St. Paul to the Galatians* (Grand Rapids, reprint ed.), pp. 58-62.

tians are commonly made the norm by which to measure the claims of other documents to have come from Paul.[4]

To reject Paul's authorship would seem to require the positing of some convincing alternative. Yet the chief candidates who might be suggested as forgers would hardly have said some of the things found in this letter. As Lightfoot[5] has pointed out, a Gnostic who wished to promote his antipathy to Judaism by using Paul's name would not have spoken deferentially of apostles of the circumcision. No Ebionite would have left an impression of disparagement regarding the customs of Jewish tradition. And if a forger were attempting to harmonize alleged Pauline and Petrine factions in the early church, he would hardly have included the incident of Galatians 2:11ff. The firm position of the Epistle to the Galatians within the Pauline corpus is without serious dissent today.

Destination

The epistle explicitly states its destination as "the churches of Galatia" (1:2), and its readers are directly addressed as "O foolish Galatians" (3:1). The name "Galatia" is derived from the Gauls or Celts who migrated to Asia Minor after earlier migrations from the Danube basin into Switzerland, South Germany, North Italy, Gaul, and Britain.[6] Their migration into Greece was repulsed at Delphi in 279 B.C., and thence three tribes (Tolistobogii, Trocmi, and Tectosages) invaded Asia Minor and harassed their new neighbors until they were ultimately confined (about 230 B.C.) to a formerly Phrygian territory around the centers of Tavium, Ancyra (Ankara, capital of modern Turkey), and Pessinus. Eventually Roman influence became strong in Asia Minor, and the Galatians learned to utilize it for their advancement. In 64 B.C. the Romans under Pompey defeated Mithridates VI, king of Pontus who had domi-

---

[4]F. F. Bruce, "Epistle to the Galatians," *New Bible Dictionary*, ed. J. D. Douglas (Grand Rapids, 1962), p. 448.

[5]Lightfoot, *Galatians*, p. 58.

[6]An excellent résumé is given by F. F. Bruce, "Galatian Problems. 2. North or South Galatians?", *Bulletin of the John Rylands Library*, vol. 52, no. 2 (Spring 1970), pp. 243-47, from which much of the above data was gleaned.

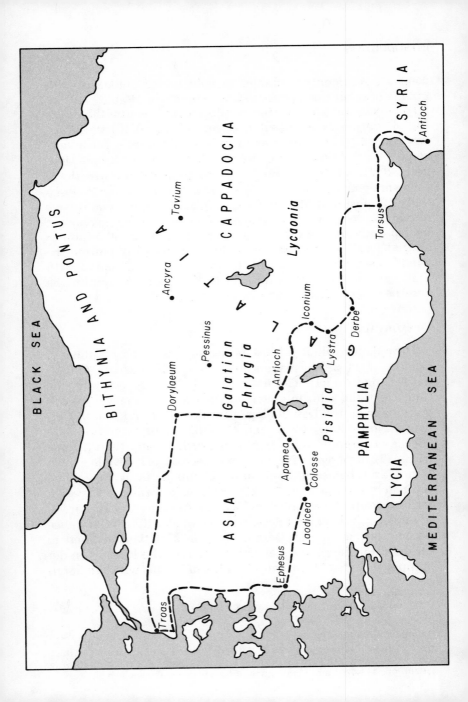

nated the area. In return for the Galatians' loyalty to Rome, Galatia was made a client kingdom, retaining this status until the death in battle of her last king, Amyntas, in 25 B.C.

The kingdom of Galatia, however, had extended itself considerably by the time of Amyntas' death. Of particular importance were such major extensions as Paphlagonia in the north, and parts of Lycaonia and Phrygia in the south, along with the cities of Pisidian Antioch, Iconium, Lystra, and Derbe. In 25 B.C. the Romans reorganized the kingdom of Galatia into an imperial province under a Roman governor.[7] This added a variety of native peoples to the Galatian tribes of the north. Paul's missionary activities in the area occurred within this political situation.

The term "Galatia" can thus be understood in two senses. It can refer to the older kingdom of Galatia, composed of Gallic peoples who had settled in the north. It can also denote the Roman province of Galatia, whose territory included the south as well.

Biblical history relating to Paul's contacts with Galatia as given in Acts reveals the following: (1) On Paul's first missionary journey, the province of Galatia was visited, but only the southern cities (Acts 13—14). (2) On the second missionary journey Galatia was again visited, including north Galatia (Acts 16:1-6). (3) On the third missionary journey, Paul again visited Galatia, but whether north Galatia was traversed depends on one's understanding of Acts 18:23.

In order to fit the Epistle to the Galatians into the historical framework of Acts, one must thus confront the question: Who are the Galatians of Paul's letter? Are they ethnic Galatians who lived in the north (but of whose churches we know nothing from Acts)? Or are they Phrygian and Lycaonian people of the south who were part of the Roman province of Galatia, whose churches had been founded on Paul's first missionary journey?

Champions of both views abound, and proof for either alternative falls short of absolute demonstration. Noteworthy

---

[7]Dio Cassius *Roman History* 53. 26. 3.

Fig. 1. Asia Minor, showing Roman provinces, cities, and major highways.

among those holding the North Galatia view is J. B. Lightfoot,[8] and this view is shared by most of the older commentators. Supporters of the South Galatia view were led by William M. Ramsay,[9] and include such recent advocates as F. F. Bruce,[10] William Hendriksen,[11] and Herman Ridderbos.[12]

Support for the North Galatia destination is usually based on the following factors: (1) Luke (in Acts) seems to use ethnographic rather than official language to describe Paul's work. It must be noted, however, that this does not demand that Paul has done the same. (2) Acts 16:6 says that Paul came to the Galatian region *after* he had visited the southern cities. (3) Luke reports nothing of a sickness during Paul's time in the southern cities, as indicated in Galatians 4:13. (4) Luke does report severe persecution in Lystra and other cities in this region, but Galatians makes no mention of this. (5) Paul would not have called the inhabitants of these southern cities "Galatians," inasmuch as ethnically they were not. It should be observed, however, that he calls others "Asians" without making ethnological distinctions (I Cor. 16:19). A comparable practice is the common nickname "Yank" for an American soldier, whether from New England or the South. (6) Lightfoot pointed to the instability of the Galatians as reflected in the epistle, to which he compared testimony in classical authors regarding the fickleness of the Gauls.[13]

Common arguments for the South Galatia destination are as follows: (1) Paul seems always to use the current political names of districts under Roman control, such as Achaia, Macedonia, Illyricum, Dalmatia, Judea, Arabia, and Asia. Of course, this does not settle the question of destination because North Galatia was also a part of the province of Galatia. (2) Acts 16:6

[8]Lightfoot, *Galatians*, pp. 18-35

[9]William M. Ramsay, *The Church in the Roman Empire* (Grand Rapids, reprint ed. 1954), pp. 97-111; *St. Paul the Traveller and Roman Citizen* (Grand Rapids, reprint ed. 1949), pp. 89-151; *A Historical Commentary on St. Paul's Epistle to the Galatians* (Grand Rapids, reprint ed. 1965), pp. 1-234.

[10]F. F. Bruce, "Galatian Problems. 2. North or South Galatians?", pp. 243-66.

[11]William Hendriksen, *Exposition of Galatians* (Grand Rapids, 1968), pp. 4-14.

[12]Ridderbos, *Galatians*, pp. 22-31.

[13]Lightfoot, *Galatians*, pp. 14-16.

can be understood to mean Galatic Phrygia, the area of Phrygia which had been incorporated into the province of Galatia.[14] (3) Luke says nothing about the founding of any churches in North Galatia. (4) Galatian churches helped in the Collection (I Cor. 16:1); yet no representatives from North Galatia are mentioned—only ones from South Galatia (Acts 20:4). This argument and the preceding one are built on Luke's silence. (5) South Galatia was more accessible to Judaizing opponents. The main highway from Syria to the West ran through the Cilician Gates at Tarsus to Iconium and Ephesus. In rebuttal, however, it could be said that these opponents could have gone anywhere they wished. If Paul could have gotten there, so could they. (6) Barnabas was Paul's companion in South Galatia, but not in North Galatia (cf. Gal. 2:13). Barnabas, however, did not need to be personally known by the readers in order for Paul to mention him (note I Cor. 9:6, where there is no evidence that the Corinthians knew him).

Ramsay, however, based his argument for the South Galatia theory not on the above propositions which fall short of certainty, but on the historical geography of Asia Minor and the lines of communication which existed in the empire.[15] The chief land routes across Asia Minor bypassed ethnic Galatia. Thus he concluded that Paul's policy would have caused him to concentrate on the main roads in the Roman provinces.

Both viewpoints are still stoutly defended, and positive proof is thus far elusive. The South Galatia view, however, has come increasingly to the fore since Ramsay's day, and is the more widely held among conservative scholars. If it is wondered why the church fathers held the North Galatia view, Bruce reminds us that Lycaonia was detached from Galatia around A.D. 137, and around A.D. 297 the remainder of South Galatia was made into a new province of Pisidia, with Pisidian Antioch as capital and Iconium as its second city. Thus in the days of the fathers, "Galatia" meant North Galatia only, and they would naturally have interpreted Galatians 1:2 in that manner.[16]

---

[14]Bruce, "Galatian Problems. 2. North or South Galatians?", pp. 255-59.
[15]Ramsay, The Church in the Roman Empire, pp. 8-11.
[16]Bruce, "Galatian Problems. 2. North or South Galatians?", p. 247.

Date

Determination of the date and place of writing of Galatians depends on the interpretation of data in the epistle itself, and the harmonization of it with the movements of Paul as given in Acts. Two items are of particular importance: (1) the implication of 4:13 that Paul had been among the Galatian churches on two occasions prior to this epistle; (2) the identification of Paul's visit to Jerusalem in 2:1-10.

Galatians 4:13 states that Paul had evangelized them "at the first," and the Greek expression (*to proteron*) can be understood as the former of two visits (in contrast to *prōtos,* which would indicate the first in a series of three or more). By this understanding, those holding the North Galatia view must place the letter sometime subsequent to Paul's passage through Galatia on his third missionary journey. The letter is commonly explained as being written from Ephesus subsequent to Acts 19:1 (A.D. 53-55). It is not certain, however, that *to proteron* must be pressed to this extent. All other New Testament uses of this expression clearly employ it in the more general sense of "formerly," where the idea of the earlier of two instances could not possibly be meant (John 6:62; 9:8; I Tim. 1:13).[17] Supporters of the South Galatia view are thus able to posit the writing of Galatians any time after the close of the first missionary journey. Even if the stricter sense of *to proteron* is followed, it seems possible to regard the statement as reflecting Paul's two visits to the Galatian churches on the first journey at the time he doubled back on his return to Antioch (Acts 14:21).

A problem of greater complexity is the identification of Paul's Jerusalem trip described in Galatians 2:1-10. Outstanding scholars have differed on this matter. J. B. Lightfoot,[18] R. C. H. Lenski,[19] and H. A. W. Meyer[20] have seen Galatians 2 as Paul's account of what went on behind the scenes at the Jerusalem

---

[17]Cf. W. F. Arndt and F. W. Gingrich, *A Greek-English Lexicon of the New Testament* (Chicago, 1957), p. 729.

[18]Lightfoot, *Galatians,* pp. 123-28.

[19]R. C. H. Lenski, *The Interpretation of St. Paul's Epistles to the Galatians, to the Ephesians, and to the Philippians* (Columbus, 1946), pp. 67-68.

[20]H. A. W. Meyer, *Critical and Exegetical Handbook to the Epistle to the Galatians* (New York, 1884), pp. 43-51.

Council in Acts 15. Others, such as W. M. Ramsay[21] and F. F. Bruce,[22] correlate Galatians 2 with Paul's Famine visit to Jerusalem in Acts 11:27-30 and 12:24-25.

Favoring the identification of Galatians 2:1-10 with the Jerusalem Council of Acts 15 are the many similarities in the accounts. (1) The same churches—Jerusalem and Antioch—are involved, and the time can be harmonized. (2) Paul, Barnabas, Peter, and James are mentioned in both accounts, along with certain unnamed disturbers. (3) The topic of Gentile circumcision is the basic issue in each account, and the same result occurred in each—Gentiles were exempted from circumcision, and the apostolic commission of Paul and Barnabas was recognized. (4) Titus (Gal. 2:3) can be understood among the "certain others" of Acts 15:2. (5) It is also noted that Galatians 2:2 is parallel to Acts 15:4, 12. (6) Sometimes it is also argued that Paul's apostolic mission was not recognized until after the Acts 11 visit (i.e., not until 13:1), whereas it seems to have been understood prior to the Galatians 2 visit.

Those favoring the identification of Galatians 2:1-10 with the Famine visit of Acts 11:27-30 and 12:24-25 can also make a plausible case. (1) The same two churches were involved, with the trip being initiated by Antioch. (2) According to the data in Galatians, the trip described in Galatians 2 is clearly Paul's second visit to Jerusalem since his conversion; and according to Acts this would have been the Famine visit. To argue as some do[23] that no apostles were in Jerusalem at this time and thus Paul ignores this visit is hardly consistent with his obvious intent of removing suspicion by recounting *all* the data (Gal. 1:20). His use of "then" (*epeita*, Gal. 2:1) leaves no hint that any trip has been omitted. (3) At the Galatians 2 visit no question was brought before the church, nor was any authoritative answer given. The "only" exhortation was that they continue remembering the poor. This fits Acts 11 better, inasmuch as Acts 15 concerned a problem and gained an official response. (4) The Acts 11 visit had only two delegates and Galatians 2 agrees, for

[21]Ramsay, *Historical Commentary on Galatians*, pp. 280-304.
[22]F. F. Bruce, *The Book of the Acts* (Grand Rapids, 1954), pp. 298-302.
[23]For example, see Lightfoot, *Galatians*, p. 127.

Titus is described in terms suggesting he was a subordinate (*sumparalabōn*, Gal. 2:1). Acts 15, however, implies that there were other delegates with Paul and Barnabas (15:2). (5) The Galatians 2 visit was made in response to divine revelation. This could be understood as a reference to the prophecy of Agabus (Acts 11:27-30). (6) The private discussion of Galatians 2 fits more easily Acts 11, than the whole church conference of Acts 15.

Against this view the problem has been raised that the matter of Gentile circumcision would not have come up again in Acts 15 if it had already been settled by the leaders in Acts 11 (Gal. 2). However, the question of Gentile circumcision arose more than once in the early church (note Acts 11:1 as well as 15:1). Furthermore, it was more likely to have arisen after a private meeting (Acts 11:27-30; Gal. 2:1-10) than after a public church conference which issued a formal statement (Acts 15). That the issue did arise again, even after Galatians 2:1-10, is clear from Galatians 2:12. It seems more reasonable to place Peter's dissimulation after a private session, than after his strong public stand taken in Acts 15.

The problem will doubtless never be solved to everyone's satisfaction. However, on the assumption that the South Galatia view of destination is correct, an early date of A.D. 49 (or thereabout), following the first missionary journey and just prior to the Jerusalem Council, provides better answers to these questions: (1) It explains why no reference is made in the epistle to the official decisions of the council. Surely they were germane to the issue under discussion, even though they were specifically addressed only to the churches of Syria and Cilicia. (2) It recognizes Galatians 2:1-10 as Paul's second visit to Jerusalem after his conversion, not his third.[24] (3) Peter's unfortunate action (Gal. 2:11 ff.) is more easily understood if it preceded the council of Acts 15.

---

[24]This is surely better than the radical suggestion of Pierson Parker, who explains that the first visit in Acts (9:26-30) is an error and never occurred; thus the Acts 15 visit actually was the second visit. "Once More, Acts and Galatians," *Journal of Biblical Literature*, vol. 86, part 2 (June 1967), pp. 175-82.

The Agitators

Reading of the epistle has convinced most interpreters that the problem which prompted the Galatian letter was the attempt by certain agitators to force the Gentile converts in these churches to observe Old Testament ceremonies and to accept a doctrine of justification on the basis of personal merit.[25] Who were these agitators? They are not named in the epistle, but certain inferences about them seem clear.

These disturbers appear to be outsiders in some sense, rather than local converts in the Galatian churches. Paul addresses the members of the churches in the second person (e.g., "ye are so soon removed," 1:6), but the agitators are referred to in the third person (e.g., "some that trouble you," 1:7; "I would they were even cut off which trouble you," 5:12).

Furthermore, the trouble was caused by more than one agitator. The plurals used in 1:7, 4:17, 5:12, and 6:12-13 clearly point in this direction. (The singular verbs and pronouns in 1:8-9, 3:1, and 5:7 can be understood as literary devices for purposes of simplification and illustration.)

It also is evident that the agitators were Judaizing Christians, and probably were from Jerusalem or were at least Jerusalem-oriented in their thinking.[26] This latter point is deduced from the character of Paul's explanations which go to considerable lengths to set forth the proper understanding of Jerusalem and its theological significance (4:21-31), as well as showing Paul's independence of Jerusalem (1:11—2:10). Robert Jewett has suggested that the situation could have arisen out of the political unrest from the Zealots in Palestine during the 40s (until the First Revolt of A.D. 66-70), in which life was dangerous for any Jews who maintained relationships with Gentiles. He argues

---

[25]F. F. Bruce has shown how all Christian interpreters until the nineteenth century understood Galatians in this way. "Galatian Problems. 3. The 'Other Gospel,' " *Bulletin of the John Rylands Library*, vol. 53, no. 2 (Spring 1971), pp. 253-71.

[26]The view of Ropes that the agitators were simply local synagogue Jews in Galatia is based on the lack of any mention that they were from Jerusalem, but does not offer as clear an explanation of the emphasis on Jerusalem in Paul's rebuttal. James Hardy Ropes, *The Singular Problem of the Epistle to the Galatians*. Harvard Theological Studies 14 (Cambridge: Harvard University Press, 1929), pp. 44-45.

that some Judean Christians had convinced themselves that circumcision of Gentile Christians would forestall Zealot reprisals.[27]

One of the puzzling features of the controversy in the Galatian churches was the presence of certain libertinistic tendencies which are difficult to harmonize with the emphasis on conformity to the Mosaic Law (5:13-26; 6:7-8). The two seem contradictory. This strange mixture occurs also in the Epistle to the Philippians (3:1-9; cf. 3:17-19). Some see two distinct groups in the congregation: one group that was enamored with the Mosaic Law and another that was reacting against it to the point of fleshly indulgence. For instance, James H. Ropes, building on an earlier theory of the German scholar Wilhelm Lutgert, suggests that the latter group was composed of a number of spiritual perfectionists whom he calls "pneumatici."[28] These disparaged Paul personally, accused him of advocating circumcision, and charged him with being subordinate to legalistic authorities in Jerusalem. Another possibility has been suggested by Jewett, who regards the problem as involving essentially one group of people. Their personal possession of the Spirit had dimmed their regard for established authority and was leading toward libertinism; at the same time they were enamored with certain cultic practices of Judaism without any real understanding of Old Testament revelation.[29] The "trappings" of religious worship are appealing to the sensual mind, and perhaps this could explain the seemingly contradictory attitudes in the congregations of Galatia. Paul, however, may have given the solution to this puzzle in Galatians 5:13, where those who have comprehended the truth that believers are free from the law are cautioned not to go to the opposite extreme and throw off all restraints. The thrust of the epistle, therefore, may be seen as directed basically

[27]Robert Jewett, "The Agitators and the Galatian Congregation," *New Testament Studies*, vol. 17, no. 2 (January 1971), pp. 204-6.

[28]Ropes, *The Singular Problem of the Epistle to the Galatians*, pp. 25-27.

[29]Jewett, "The Agitators and the Galatian Congregation," pp. 210-12.

to one group, who needed instruction as well as a cautioning against leaving the path of truth for either extreme.[30]

Outline

Opening Remarks (1:1-9)
    A. Greeting (1:1-5)
    B. Occasion and Theme (1:6-9)
   I. Paul's Authority Defended (1:10—2:21)
    A. The Source of Paul's Authority (1:10-17)
    B. Paul's First Trip to Jerusalem (1:18-24)
    C. Paul's Second Trip to Jerusalem (2:1-10)
    D. Paul's Encounter with Peter at Antioch (2:11-21)

  II. True Doctrine Explained (3:1—4:31)
    A. The Galatians' Previous Christian Experience (3:1-14)
    B. The Relation of the Law to the Abrahamic Covenant (3:15-22)
    C. The Relation of the Law to Christian Faith (3:23—4:7)
    D. The Folly of Returning to the Law (4:8-20)
    E. The Allegory of Abraham's Two Sons (4:21-31)

  III. Christian Practice Exhorted (5:1—6:10)
    A. Exhortation to Hold on to Freedom (5:1-12)
    B. Exhortation to Walk by the Spirit (5:13-26)
    C. Exhortation to Fulfill Responsibilities to Others (6:1-10)

Concluding Summary (6:11-18)

---

[30]F. F. Bruce, "Galatian Problems. 3. The 'Other Gospel,' " *Bulletin of the John Rylands Library*, vol. 53, no. 2 (Spring 1971), pp. 260-61.

Chapter 1

Opening Remarks

(Galatians 1:1-9)

The Epistle to the Galatians begins in the usual style of ancient letters by naming the writer, the addressee(s), and conveying some word of greeting. In Paul's letters these formalities are never mere stereotypes, but are consciously molded to fit the circumstances. Usually he adds a thanksgiving or prayer for his readers, often recalling some specific incident or characteristic which had endeared them to him. In this instance, however, such commendation is conspicuously absent. The apostle is deeply disturbed and plunges abruptly into the issue which required direct confrontation. Even the opening words are not his most common description of himself but seem to be a response to attacks made against him.

A. Greeting (1:1-5)

1. *The writer.* (1:1-2a)

VERSE 1. The author designates himself as Paul, the Roman name of Saul of Tarsus which is used consistently of him in the New Testament after his labors began taking him into Gentile areas (Acts 13:9). Terming himself an apostle (as he does also in the opening remarks in Romans, I and II Corinthians, Ephesians, Colossians, I and II Timothy, and Titus), he proceeds to clarify just what sort of apostle he is. Surely the false insinuations of the Judaizers in Galatia must have prompted this precise explanation. By the use of two prepositions "of" and "by" (KJV),[1] Paul asserted that his right to be an apostle was not granted to him by any man or group of men. The first phrase is literally "not from men," and states that the ultimate source of apostleship was not to be traced to human authority. The second phrase, "neither by man," uses a preposition that denotes intermediate

---

[1] Greek: *apo, dia.*

agency.[2] Some might have conceded that ultimately God had called him, but that the Twelve in Jerusalem were the human agents who appointed him, and thus his apostleship was of a lesser order than theirs. Paul states with no uncertainty that man was neither the ultimate source nor even the intermediate agent.

From the reading of Acts 9:1-22 one might wonder how Paul could say that his commission did not come "through" a man in view of the actions of Ananias who brought the divine commission to him. However, it is clear that Ananias was nothing more than God's spokesman on that occasion. He possessed no authority of his own which would have made him superior to Paul. Even Paul's enemies apparently never tried to cite the action of Ananias in a way that would downgrade Paul.

In strong contrast[3] to any thoughts of mere human authorization, Paul's apostleship came "through Jesus Christ and God the Father." Here the preposition (dia) which denotes the agent is used because the risen Christ, in association with the Father who had raised Him, was the One who had bestowed on Paul the ministry of an apostle. Paul does not find it necessary to use also the other word to show ultimate source (apo), for there is no higher being who could have utilized Christ and the Father as agents. In this instance the source and agent of Paul's commissioning coincided in Christ and the Father.

VERSE 2a. "All the brethren which are with me" is probably a reference to Paul's coworkers, not just fellow Christians (cf. Phil. 4:21-22, where the same expression is used in distinction from the rest of the Christians). They were not cowriters of the letter, however, for Paul very quickly begins writing in the first person (1:6). It was the habit of the apostle to include his associates in his opening greeting, even though it was evident that he alone was the writer of the letter. Identification of these brethren is dependent on one's view of the place of writing. The view advanced in these studies (see Introduction, "Date") postulates the writing as from Syrian Antioch after the close of the first

---

[2]Greek: dia.

[3]The strong adversative alla (but) points up the great contrast between the alternatives.

Fig. 2. Site of Pisidian Antioch, the first city of South Galatia visited by Paul and Barnabas on the First Missionary Journey. *Kelsey*

missionary journey. The "brethren" would then have included Barnabas, and perhaps the other leaders of the Antioch church (Acts 13:1).

2. The addressees. (1:2b)

VERSE 2b. "Unto the churches of Galatia" indicates the first readers to be members of a number of local churches in Galatia. The probability is that these were the congregations at Pisidian Antioch (Fig. 2), Iconium (Fig. 9), Lystra (Fig. 11), and Derbe (Fig. 14), located in the Roman province of Galatia (see Fig. 1, and Introduction, "Destination"). They had been founded on the first missionary journey by Paul and Barnabas. These four cities were located on the main commercial and military route that connected Syria with the West.[4] The plural "churches" (ekklēsiais) is in interesting contrast to the singular form "church" (ekklēsian) in 1:13, showing that Paul's concept was of various congregations which were local manifestations of the one spiritual unity, the church of God, called sometimes the body of Christ (Eph. 4:12; Col. 1:24).

3. The blessing. (1:3-5)

VERSE 3. The twin blessings of grace and peace are the same as those given to the Romans (1:7), Corinthians (I Cor. 1:3; II Cor. 1:2), Ephesians (1:2), Philippians (1:2), Colossians (1:2), Thessalonians (I Thess. 1:1; II Thess. 1:2), and Philemon (3). Paul was greatly concerned about his readers' spiritual condition, and expresses no word of thanksgiving about reports he has received. Nevertheless, he has not abandoned hope that the Galatians were truly saved and would ultimately see the danger of their position. Thus he desires for them the favor of God from which all blessings flow, and the experiencing of the peace of God which brings assurance to the heart (Phil. 4:7). The usual epistolary greeting among Greek writers was chairein (Acts 23:26; James 1:1), but Paul has altered it to charis (grace), with all

---

[4]G. Ernest Wright, Biblical Archaeology (Philadelphia, 1962), p. 254; William M. Ramsay, A Historical Commentary on St. Paul's Epistle to the Galatians (Grand Rapids, reprint ed., 1965), p. 184.

the richness with which Christian understanding has ennobled the word. "Peace" (eirēnē), on the other hand, was the Greek rendering of the familiar Hebrew greeting shālom. Whether or not Paul was deliberately using the greetings of two cultures, it is surely to be understood that he employed both terms in a thoroughly Christian sense to desire God's best for his converts in Galatia.

VERSES 4-5. These blessings of grace and peace would proceed from God the Father and the Lord Jesus Christ (v. 3). Only because of what these Persons of the Godhead did, are such blessings possible. Each of these Persons is described in inverted sequence (a grammatical construction called chiasmus). It was Christ who gave Himself for man's sins. Here Paul initiates the theme which the rest of the epistle will elaborate—that sins were cared for in their entirety by Christ, not partly by a system of human law-keeping. An understanding of this truth cuts the ground from beneath all legalism.

In giving Himself to deal with sins, Christ's ultimate purpose was to rescue sinners from this present evil world. The verb "deliver" (exelētai), when in the middle voice as here, is always used in the New Testament with the sense of rescuing from danger (Acts 7:10, 34; 12:11; 23:27; 26:17). The term "world" (aiōnos) means here not the physical earth, but the world period or age, with all that characterizes it. The specific age in view is the present temporal one (enestōtos), which is actively evil (ponērou) and in which every man is captive to sin unless he is rescued by the saving work of Christ. This rescue does not refer to some future deliverance at death or the second coming of Christ, but should be understood as already accomplished by the forgiveness of sins and the bestowal of eternal life.[5]

God the Father is the One by whose will the plan of redemption was conceived and effected. In the loving desire of "our God and Father"[6] the Savior was sent (John 3:16). Again the apostle has stated that the means of salvation is not to be found in man's efforts, but in God's gracious will and plan. No wonder, then,

---

[5] The verb "rescued" (exelētai) should be regarded as an effective aorist.

[6] The one article with the expression tou theou kai patros hēmōn supports this rendering as preferable to the ambiguous "God and our Father" (KJV).

that he exults in these concluding words of praise: "To whom be the glory for ever and ever. Amen." He does not mean merely that men ought to bestow praise or glory on God (although, of course, they should), but that glory is what God possesses in His own being, and this glory should be acknowledged by grateful men as they see His glory demonstrated in His saving of men.

B. Occasion and Theme (1:6-9)

1. *The Galatians are in process of deserting to a different gospel.* (1:6-7)

VERSE 6. Instead of words of thanksgiving which usually appear in Paul's letters at this point, the apostle goes immediately to the problem which prompted the letter. He was amazed that the Galatians were so quickly turning aside from the purity of the gospel which once they had received. The expression "so soon" or "so quickly" (*houtōs tacheōs*) may have reference to the recentness of their conversion, or to Paul's recent visit among them, or perhaps to the recent arrival of the Judaizers.

The Galatians are accused by Paul of actually being in the process of deserting from God. The verb[7] describing their action stresses two facts: (1) The middle voice shows that the Galatians themselves were blamable for what was happening: "ye are removing yourselves," or "ye are deserting." Even though the Judaizing teachers may have been chiefly at fault, the Galatians were allowing themselves to be swayed by this faulty doctrine, and so could not be totally absolved of blame. They were not forced to listen to false teaching. They should have compared what they heard with the truth which had been taught them by the apostolic missionaries and their faithful leaders since. To continue listening to unreliable teachers was to court disaster. (2) The present tense of the verb indicates that this desertion was not yet an accomplished fact. They were engaged in doing it, but it had not yet been fully done. Already some were observing Jewish religious festivals (4:10), but none of them had as yet adopted circumcision (5:2). Paul's earnest hope was that by this letter he would be successful in arresting this alarming trend and reversing it toward the true gospel of Christ.

---

[7]Greek: *metatithesthe.*

In Paul's eyes the insistence that Mosaic requirements should be added to faith in Christ's work of grace as necessary for salvation was not merely a minor sectarian deviation. It was actually a deserting from "him that called you." The reference is to God, by whose effective call men are brought to salvation through Christ. In Paul's writings this sort of "call" is invariably used of the act of God whose call to men is always successful.[8] Paul assumes that the Galatians have truly responded to the gospel and were saved, but apostolic warnings are always in order, for it is by such means that God keeps His children faithful, and obedience to God's Word demonstrates the reality of one's faith (I John 2:3-5). The Judaizers, of course, would have insisted that they were not promoting any desertion from the God who saves men. Yet if the truth of God's promise is adulterated, followers of that corrupted message are not really obeying God at all. The same charge is hurled at Judaizing teachers elsewhere (cf. Heb. 3:12).

VERSE 7. Such confusion of legalism with grace is a "different gospel" (*heteron euangelion*). The translation "another gospel which is not another" (KJV) is confusing because it renders two different Greek words by the same English word "another." The tendency among scholars today is to regard the words *heteros* and *allos* as synonyms, and thus to deny any recognizable difference between them in Koine.[9] The distinction then becomes only literary, not conceptual. Paul is understood to say that this "other gospel" is really no gospel at all, except in the opinion of the Judaizing troublemakers.

However, it should be noted that classical Greek did make a distinction between these words, with *heteros* denoting a difference in kind.[10] While it is claiming too much to draw a sharp distinction in all cases, instances where both appear in the same

---

[8]The Pauline uses of *kaleō* and *klēsis* with the meaning of God's call to men for salvation are: Rom. 4:17; 8:30; 9:11, 24; I Cor. 1:9; 7:15, 17, 18(2), 20, 21, 22, 24; Gal. 1:6, 15; 5:8, 13; Eph. 4:1, 4; Col. 3:15; I Thess. 2:12; 4:7; 5:24; II Thess. 2:14; I Tim. 6:12; II Tim. 1:9.

[9]W. F. Arndt and F. W. Gingrich, *A Greek-English Lexicon of the New Testament* (Chicago, 1957), p. 315; H. W. Beyer, "Heteros," *Theological Dictionary of the New Testament*, ed. Gerhard Kittel, trans. Geoffrey W. Bromiley (Grand Rapids, 1964), 2, 702-4.

[10]TDNT, 2, 702.

context suggest that the differences rather than the similarities of the terms may be significant. If differences are to be seen, then *heteros* distinguishes between different kinds, and *allos* adds another of the same general sort.[11] By this view Paul is understood to say that the Judaizers' teaching is really a different kind of "gospel," not just another of the same sort. There is a fundamental difference between the message of salvation through the free provision of grace in Christ, and a system which gives some place to human works.

This legalistic teaching was a "gospel" only in the eyes of its advocates. These troublers were still active in Galatia and were continually agitating the Galatian believers. They are called *hoi tarassontes*, a word which literally meant to shake together or stir up (as in John 5:4), and figuratively to throw into confusion, whether by outward tumult (Acts 17:8) or mental agitation (Acts 15:24). Surely it was disturbing for Paul's Gentile converts in Galatia to be told that trusting Christ for salvation was insufficient to save them. Yet to insist on imposing the requirements of Judaism was to pervert the gospel of Christ, for it would change its basic character from that of a gift from God to one of merit derived from human works.

2. *Any who promote a different gospel are under the curse of God.* (1:8-9)

VERSE 8.   Not only is the false message to be shunned, but the promoters of untruth must be recognized for what they are. No matter how impressive the messenger may be, the all-important issue is the message. Paul illustrated this by the hypothetical possibility[12] that even if he or his associates ("we") or an angel from heaven should preach some other "gospel," the criterion for accepting their message was not the credentials of the messenger but the content of the message. By pointing to relatively unimpeachable sources as angels or his own missionary party who nevertheless will be judged on the basis of their fidelity to the truth, Paul did not need to impugn directly the less worthy

---

[11]J. B. Lightfoot states the rule: "Thus *allos* adds, while *heteros* distinguishes." *The Epistle of St. Paul to the Galatians* (Grand Rapids, reprint ed.), p. 76.

[12]The conditional clause employs *ean* with the subjunctive, indicating that the condition is not presently realized, and is thus only hypothetical.

Judaizers. If even Paul or an angel could not escape judgment if they perverted the doctrine of salvation by grace, how much more must the Judaizers be in danger of divine retribution.

Translations vary in their handling of *par' ho* in characterizing the false evangelizing as "other than" (KJV) or "contrary to" (NASB) the preaching which had been given to the readers by Paul. From the basic meaning of the word which meant "beside" or "alongside of," there developed a comparative use: "beyond" or "more than." In contexts where this involved a going beyond proper limits, the adversative meaning "contrary to" is also legitimate. In Galatians 1:8 Paul means that any proclamation of salvation which goes beyond God's revelation of grace is actually opposed to the true gospel. Hence the meanings of "beyond" and "contrary to" converge in this instance.

Angels may have been mentioned by Paul because the Judaizing agitators were stressing the fact of angelic involvement in the giving of the Mosaic Law (3:19; Acts 7:53; Heb. 2:2). Perhaps he was also reminding them that Satan may pose as an angel of light (II Cor. 11:14). There could also be a remembrance of what had happened on Paul's first visit to the Galatian city of Lystra, when the superstitious populace at first thought Paul and Barnabas themselves were supernatural visitors (Acts 14:11-12).

"Let him be accursed" is Paul's strong expression describing the consequences to perverters of the gospel. It does not mean excommunication from the church, for the term *anathema*[13] is used here regarding an angel and elsewhere even by blasphemers regarding Jesus (I Cor. 12:3). Comparison with other New Testament uses indicates that the word involved the delivering of someone to the destructive judgment of God. Such a person is "away from Christ" (*apo tou Christou*, Rom. 9:3), and thus is consigned to everlasting punishment (II Thess. 1:9). Of course, Paul is not actually passing judgment, for God alone does this, but he is agreeing with God's righteous judgment to

---

[13]*Anathema.* is a Hellenistic form for the classical *anathēma*. It was used of something devoted to deity, whether as a consecrated offering laid up in the temple or as delivered up to divine wrath (J. Behm, "Anathema, *et al.*," *TDNT*, 1, 854-55). In the NT *anathema* is reserved for "curse," and the related form *anathēma* denotes the votive offering (Luke 21:5). *Anathema* is thus similar to the Hebrew *hērem* in such passages as Num. 21:3; Deut. 7:26; Josh. 6:17; 7:12; Judg. 1:17; Zech. 14:11.

come which will eventually carry out such a sentence against perverters of His truth.

VERSE 9. In concluding this introductory statement, Paul repeats a warning which had been made previously to the Galatians.[14] This time, in distinction from the grammatical form of the statement in 1:8, Paul constructs the sentence in a way which assumes that the condition was presently occurring.[15] Therefore, he does not say "we" (he knew that he and Barnabas were not doing this) but "anyone." It should not be supposed, however, that this extreme denunciation of the legalists was a temperamental outburst against rivals. Rather it was an echo of the attitude of Jesus who spoke in similarly harsh terms against the legalists among the Pharisees (Matt. 23:13-39). A contrary gospel is in reality no gospel at all.

The ringing words of Paul should cause every reader to consider most carefully the purity of the gospel which he receives and promotes. It is no small matter. The eternal destiny of man is at stake. If we do not feel as deeply about it as did Paul, perhaps we have not understood the issues as clearly as he.

Questions for Discussion

1. In what ways has Christ delivered believers from the present evil world?
2. Why is the source of Paul's apostleship important?
3. In what sense is legalism "another gospel"?
4. Why does the adding of Mosaic requirements pervert the gospel of Christ?
5. What is the Christian's responsibility today when the gospel is not clearly taught by many preachers and churches?

---

[14]It is not likely that Paul refers to the previous statement of 1:8, for he would hardly have shifted from "we" to "I" in the same sentence, nor would "now again" draw such a fine temporal distinction from the sentence just before. More probably "we said before" (proeirēkamen) refers to warnings to the Galatians against false teaching which were voiced by Paul and Barnabas on their previous visit.

[15]A first class condition employing ei with the indicative.

Paul's Authority Defended

(Galatians 1:10–2:21)

Chapter 2

The Source of Paul's Authority

(Galatians 1:10-24)

The question of authority is basic to the proper settlement of any conflict. A contest without referees can produce hopeless chaos. Force does not determine what is right if one is concerned about moral values. Certainly this is true regarding the gospel. If it were only a human philosophy, then its number of adherents or its beneficial results might be appealed to as authenticating its truth. But the gospel which Paul preached claimed to be a revelation from God to man, authorized by God Himself, founded on the person and work of Christ, and disseminated by apostles whom Christ had chosen. Christ, however, was no longer bodily present, and there were false apostles (II Cor. 11:13). The question was being raised in Galatia whether Paul was really an apostle on a par with the Twelve from Jerusalem. The matter is not of significance only for the historian. The epistles of Paul have shaped the faith of Christians for twenty centuries. The question of Paul's authorization is as important to believers today as it was to those of Galatia. Only if it is true that his authority came from Christ can we be sure that he has conveyed to the church the unique revelation to which it is proper, wise, and safe to commit one's life and destiny.

I. PAUL'S AUTHORITY DEFENDED (1:10—2:21)

A. The Source of Paul's Authority (1:10-17)

1. *Paul's present activity shows him to be Christ's servant, not man's.* (1:10)

VERSE 10. In the background of this question asked by Paul in 1:10, there must lie the reports given to him that some were attacking his apostleship, accusing him particularly of changing his message to win the favor of whatever audience he chanced to have at the time. Perhaps they were saying that when Paul moved in Jewish circles he preached compliance with circumcision and the Mosaic Law, but that when he had come to Galatia he had softened his message by dropping the Mosaic requirements so as to be more popular among the Gentiles and to win more followers. On another occasion Paul was similarly charged with writing strong letters from a distance but being weak and conciliatory when he was actually present (II Cor. 10:1, 10). Such an accusation completely missed the point of Paul's policy of expediency (I Cor. 9:20-22), which was willing to accept all sorts of personal inconvenience as long as the gospel itself was not compromised.[1]

Having heard what was being said about him, Paul asks, "At this moment is it men I am trying to gain the approval of[2] or God?" "At this moment" (arti) has the emphatic position in the sentence and calls our attention to the anathema just written in 1:8-9. Surely no one could say Paul was trying to ingratiate himself with men at this moment. It should be clear to the readers that he would not have written as harshly as he did if human reaction to his words were his uppermost concern.

Paul answered his own question by asserting that he would not be Christ's servant if he were still a popularity seeker.[3] If he had changed his message to win more human favor, then he would have been unfaithful to his apostleship. The employment of "yet" (eti) in the clause "if I yet pleased men," calls attention to some previous period of his life when he did seek to please men, either actually or as alleged by his opponents. Inasmuch as Paul would hardly have characterized any part of his Christian life as not involving his being a servant of Christ, it is better to

---

[1]Those who date Galatians subsequent to the Jerusalem Council point to Paul's circumcision of Timothy as an incident to which the Judaizers might have referred in charging him with inconsistency (Acts 16:1-3).

[2]The Greek verb is peithō, which is more commonly rendered "persuade." However, the idea of "persuading God" is difficult, and it is better to regard the precise sense of peithō here as indicated by the parallel verb areskein, to please; hence peithō here is "to conciliate, win over, strive to please" (Arndt, pp. 644-45).

[3]The grammar indicates a contrary-to-fact condition, both clauses being assumed as untrue by the speaker.

view the "yet" as in contrast either to the charges made against him (just as "at this moment" earlier in the verse) or else to his pre-Christian life when he did seek to win personal advancement as a young Pharisee (1:14). It is obvious, therefore, that Paul's dedication to his apostleship (1:1) contained an awareness on his part that this required him to be Christ's servant. His willingness to anathematize some men, if need be, was a demonstration of his wholehearted allegiance to Christ.

2. *His gospel was revealed to him by Christ, not mere man.*
   (1:11-12)

VERSE 11. In a most solemn manner Paul asserted the source of his apostleship. "I certify" *(gnōrizō)*, he says, that the message of saving good news which he had brought to them was not "according to man" *(kata anthrōpon)*. It was not to be measured or accounted for by human standards, either as to its origin or its development.

VERSE 12. Neither had Paul received it from any other man by means of human tradition handed down from the past. The word "received" *(parelabon)* was the regular term for receiving transmitted material (I Cor. 11:23; 15:1; Gal. 1:9; Phil. 4:9; I Thess. 2:13; 4:1; II Thess. 3:6). Furthermore, Paul had not "been taught" *(edidachthēn)* the gospel by any school or formal instruction by the Twelve. Even Ananias, whom the Lord sent to him in Damascus (Acts 9:10-19) did not teach him the gospel. Most believers do receive the gospel this way, but Paul claims that this was not his experience.

Paul received the gospel as a direct revelation from Jesus Christ, just as in the case of the Twelve. He does not elaborate, except to deny that there was any human agent. Not only did he speak with the glorified Jesus Christ directly on the Damascus road (Acts 9:1-9), but he also was granted other revelations (II Cor. 12:1-11). It should not be forgotten that even the Twelve received their full understanding of Christ's teaching by the Holy Spirit after Christ had ascended (John 14:26; 16:13-15).

3. *One proof is seen in Paul's past life in Judaism.* (1:13-14)

VERSE 13. In demonstration of his claim that no human agency was responsible for providing him with the message he preached, Paul cited first his pre-Christian career in Judaism. He stated that his readers had previously "heard" (ēkousate) of his earlier activities. Perhaps he himself had recounted the remarkable story of his conversion when he had been among them. He told his experience in considerable detail several times in Scripture (Acts 22:1-16; 26:1-20), and stated his belief that his case was intended by God to serve as a pattern of God's longsuffering (I Tim. 1:12-16). Or it may have been that his opponents had informed the Galatians about him.

Paul's manner of life[4] in Judaism certainly had not taught him the gospel. On the contrary, during that period of his life he was engaged[5] in his vicious persecuting activities against those who had already believed the gospel. It was while he was observing Jewish traditions that he launched his attacks against the church, supposing in his spiritual blindness that he was actually protecting the Old Testament faith. In describing his actions, he does not spare himself, for he used the same word "wasted" (KJV) or "was ravaging" (eporthoun) as did the Damascenes when they described his activities (Acts 9:21).

Although the Epistle to the Galatians was written early in the Christian era, it is clear that already the apostle has the concept of a spiritual unity of believers which he calls "the church of God" (tēn ekklēsian tou theou), as well as localized "churches" (1:2, ekklēsiais), and that these are to be distinguished in some manner from "Judaism" (Ioudaismōi).

VERSE 14. Paul's claim of a rapid rise above his peers in traditional Jewish circles is confirmed by the Biblical record. As a young man he apparently assumed the leadership of the persecution following Stephen's death (Acts 8:1, 3; cf. 7:58). He showed his unusual zeal[6] by not confining his persecuting

---

[4]The Greek term anastrophē denotes conduct or behavior. The KJV rendering "conversation" once meant this, but it is now an obsolete use of the English word.

[5]The verbs ediōkon (persecuting) and eporthoun (ravaging) are both imperfect indicatives, emphasizing the continuing activity of Paul.

[6]The use of the word zēlōtēs caused J. B. Lightfoot to identify Paul as a member of the Zealots, which he explained as an extreme group of Pharisees (The Epistle of St. Paul to the Galatians, Grand Rapids, reprint ed., pp. 81-82). However, there is no proof that a Pharisee could also be a political Zealot, and it is more likely that Paul uses the word in a nonpolitical sense as "a zealot for Jewish traditions."

efforts to Jerusalem but by seeking to extradite those who had escaped the city and fled to Damascus (Acts 9:1).

The "traditions of my fathers" are probably not a reference merely to the Mosaic institutions which were the core of Old Testament religion, but refer to the "traditions of the elders" (Matt. 15:2; Mark 7:3, 5). These were the Jewish oral laws devised to apply the written law to new circumstances. These traditions are known today as the Halachah, and are collected in the Talmud. Jesus often disregarded these rabbinical interpretations because they actually undermined or violated the true intent of Scripture (Mark 7:13). Thus Paul's avid promotion of Jewish traditions in his pre-Christian life was hardly the explanation of the source of his message, for his gospel was diametrically opposed to that which he had once espoused.

4. *Another proof is seen in Paul's earliest Christian activity.* (1:15-17)

VERSE 15. Even Paul's conversion and his earliest Christian experience did not supply any human source for his gospel message. It was God[7] whose sovereign act marked out[8] Paul for salvation and service even before his birth. God's successful call produced Paul's response on the Damascus road.

VERSE 16. "To reveal his Son in me" points to the inward revelation to Paul which brought about his new birth. Although some have interpreted this statement to mean that God wanted to reveal His Son through Paul to the Gentiles,[9] it is much more likely that the revelation is to Paul himself. The phrase is "in me" (*en emoi*), not "through me" (*di' emou*). Furthermore, this accords with the usual sense of *apokalupto*, which denotes a subjective revelation taking place in the mind of the person and resulting in knowledge on his part (I Cor. 2:10; 14:30; Eph. 3:5).[10] Assuming that it means a revelation to Paul, when did it

---

[7]"God" does not appear in many ancient texts, but it is clear from the mention of "his Son" in 1:16 that God is meant. When the verb *eudokeo* (please) is used of God in the NT, it always denotes His sovereign will as operating.

[8]"Marked out" or "separated" (*aphorisas*) does not refer to the act of physical birth (i.e., separated from the womb), but "separated to God" from the time of his birth. The thought and wording is similar to Jer. 1:5.

[9] J. B. Lightfoot, *Galatians*, pp. 82-83.

[10]E. D. Burton, *The Epistle to the Galatians* (Edinburgh, reprint ed., 1971), pp. 49-51, 433-35.

occur? Did it come to him entirely on the Damascus road, or did
Ananias convey part of it to him? Acts 9:15 and 22:13-16 might
suggest that Ananias gave the message to Paul. However, a
comparison with Acts 26:13-18 indicates that Paul had been told
much of this information by the Lord before Ananias came to
him. Hence Ananias should be understood as confirming to Paul
in more calm circumstances what Paul had already been told in
his vision. It should also be remembered that Paul had been
alone for three days after the vision before Ananias came to him,
and thus had considerable opportunity for further revelation.

The purpose of this revelation given to Paul was that he might
proclaim the gospel among the Gentiles. The ministry among
Gentiles as well as Jews was specifically mentioned in his commission (Acts 9:15). Paul did not regard his ministry as restricted to Gentiles (anymore than Peter preached only to Jews),
and his usual procedure was to preach in synagogues in the
cities he visited, but he understood that primarily he was the
apostle to the uncircumcised (Gal. 2:8, 9).

Following his initial revelation from God, Paul did not confer
with "flesh and blood," that is, with any human authorities who
might issue orders to him. "Flesh and blood" reminds us of
Christ's words to Peter that "flesh and blood" had not revealed
the true identity of Jesus to him (Matt. 16:17). Thus Paul claimed
the same source of revelation regarding Christ as Peter had. No
Christian in Damascus, not even Ananias, was consulted so as to
provide instruction or grant any sort of authorization to him.

VERSE 17. Neither did he go to Jerusalem in those early days
after his conversion. The emphasis on Jerusalem here and in the
following verses probably reflects the opponents' claim that
Jerusalem was really the headquarters of true doctrine, and that
Paul must be subordinate to the Jerusalem apostles. Paul does
not disparage the Twelve who had been apostles before he had
been appointed by Christ, but merely says he did not see them at
this time.

Instead he had gone to Arabia. This visit, not recorded in Acts,
must have occurred during Acts 9:20-27, and probably between
9:22 and 23. It cannot be determined what part of the wide area
called Arabia is meant. In New Testament times the Arabian
kingdom of the Nabateans reached to the vicinity of Damascus

(see Fig. 3); so one need not imagine a long trip to the Sinai peninsula. A more accessible place near Damascus is rendered probably by the mention of the Nabatean king Aretas whose ethnarch at Damascus was active in the plot against Paul (II Cor. 11:32, 33), and also by the fact that Paul returned to Damascus afterward. The purpose of Paul's trip to Arabia is not stated, nor its length; but it seems more likely that it was for meditation than for preaching.

Still Paul had not contacted any apostles. There were none at Damascus, and when he left for a time it was to go to Arabia, and then he returned once more to Damascus. His message, therefore, came from no human authorities, not even from the Twelve at Jerusalem, but from the divine Father who had revealed His Son.

B. Paul's First Trip to Jerusalem (1:18-24)

1. *After three years Paul went to Jerusalem.* (1:18-20)

VERSE 18. Paul did eventually visit Jerusalem after his conversion, and therefore he must show whether this visit impinged on his claim of independence from the Twelve. "After three years" is probably to be computed from the time of his conversion.[11] Lest it be charged against him that it was this trip which provided him with his instruction in the gospel and his apostleship, Paul clearly stated that the purpose of the visit was "to become acquainted with Cephas."[12] That he should desire to meet this leading apostle (more commonly known by his Greek name, Peter, John 1:42) is hardly surprising. This was not a lengthy visit, however, for it lasted only fifteen days. There is an

---

[11]The constructing of a detailed NT chronology is rendered difficult by the lack of precise data. In this instance it is not certain whether the three years are to be regarded as three full years (36 months), or as a round number to indicate more than two years (during the third year), or as one full year plus portions of the years immediately preceding and following.

[12]The Aramaic name Cephas is used in the NT only in the writings of Paul (I Cor. 1:12; 3:22; 9:5; 15:5; Gal. 1:18; 2:9, 11, 14), except for the instance when Jesus bestowed the name on Simon son of Jona (John 1:42). The more familiar Greek name Peter occurs 153 times in the NT, but only twice is it used by Paul (Gal. 2:7, 8).

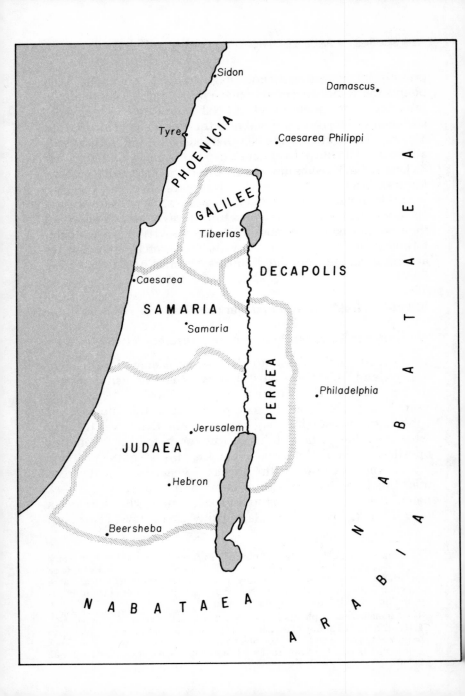

indication in the word "abode" or "stayed" (*epemeina*) that Paul's stay had to be prolonged[13] in order to get to see Peter (i.e., he "stayed over"). If this should be the correct inference of the statement, Acts, 9:26-27 may indicate the reason: the disciples in Jerusalem (including Peter) were afraid of him at first.

VERSE 19. On this visit to Jerusalem Paul saw no other apostle "except James" (*ei mē Iakōbon*). Does this mean that James the Lord's brother[14] was an apostle? The expression *ei mē* can mark a true exception (for example, Matt. 11:27). This James, however, was not one of the Twelve, and thus was not an apostle in the special sense that Peter was. Hence it may be more likely that *ei mē* should be treated as "but" (as in Luke 4:26, 27, where the widow of Sarepta and Naaman the Syrian were not exceptions but contrasts to the statements about widows and lepers in Israel). Thus Paul is understood to say that he saw no other apostle than Peter, but he did see one additional leading figure in Jerusalem, namely, James the Lord's brother. But he could be termed an apostle only in the wider sense of those who were close associates of the Twelve. He is mentioned here because of his prominence in Jewish Christianity.

A more complete reconstruction of the events of the first visit to Jerusalem is possible by comparing Galatians with Acts 9:23-30, 22:17-21, and II Corinthians 11:32-33. Paul left Damascus because of a plot against his life. His Jewish enemies in the city were able to enlist the support of the governor appointed by the Nabatean king Aretas, and the gates of the city were kept

---

[13]F. Rendall points out that the verb *epimenō* in Acts and the Pauline epistles denotes the prolongation of a stay, and that *epemeina pros auton* is not the same as *epemeina par' autōi* ("The Epistle to the Galatians," *EGT*, 3, 155). Arndt, however, does not hesitate to equate the phrases (p. 296).

[14]The most obvious sense of this description understands James as a son of Joseph and Mary, and thus a uterine brother of Jesus. In the fourth century this view was defended by Helvidius of Rome, in opposition to Epiphanius who argued that the "brothers" of Jesus were actually sons of Joseph from a previous marriage. Jerome propounded the view that the brothers of Jesus were His first cousins, the sons of Alphaeus by Mary of Clopas whom he erroneously concluded to be the sister of the Virgin (John 19:25). See J. B. Lightfoot, "The Brethren of the Lord," *Galatians*, pp. 252-91; F. F. Bruce, *The Book of the Acts* (Grand Rapids, 1954), pp. 44-45.

Fig. 3. Palestine and Arabia.

under surveillance. Disciples whom Paul had gained[15] in the city helped him escape by lowering him through a window in the city wall by means of a basket. On arriving in Jerusalem he tried to gain access to the disciples but they were suspicious of treachery until Barnabas (the "son of encouragement," Acts 4:36) came to his aid and acted as his sponsor by introducing him to the apostles. Mention of the plural "apostles" (Acts 9:27) does not contradict Galatians 1:19, for Luke's account elsewhere uses the term *apostles* in the wider sense to include Barnabas (Acts 14:4, 14), and Paul apparently includes Silas as such (I Thess. 2:6). His brief time in Jerusalem was ended by another plot against his life (Acts 9:29), and a vision of the Lord in the temple instructing him to leave (Acts 22:17-21).

VERSE 20. This brief sketch of Paul's trip to see Peter at Jerusalem is concluded with the solemn affirmation of its truthfulness, "Behold, before God, I lie not." It seems clear, therefore, that what Paul has just written was not merely a biographical statement, but was prompted by accusations against him. He has answered the charges by explaining that he had had only the most meager contacts with the Twelve up to this time, although he had already been preaching effectively in Damascus. Furthermore, his chief contacts at Jerusalem had been two men whose emphasis was particularly Jewish—Peter and James! They would hardly have provided him with a different gospel which misrepresented the Mosaic Law!

2. Following this, Paul went to Syria and Cilicia. (1:21-24)

VERSE 21. The first postconversion trip of Paul to Jerusalem was cut short by the plot against him and the divine command to leave the city (Acts 9:29; 22:17-21). The Acts account explains that the Christians in Jerusalem took him to Caesarea and then sent him off to Tarsus (9:29). Paul's own description says he went to "the regions of Syria and Cilicia." These "regions" (*klimata*) were various districts or small areas which made up the Roman province of Syria-Cilicia.[16] Cilicia was a part of the

---

[15]The Greek text in Acts 9:25 reads "his disciples."

[16]W. M. Ramsay, *A Historical Commentary on St. Paul's Epistle to the Galatians* (Grand Rapids, reprint ed., 1965), pp. 275-80.

province of Syria from 38 B.C. to A.D. 72.[17] Inasmuch as the Acts narrative mentions Paul's going to Tarsus (in Cilicia) before his going to Antioch (in Syria), one may wonder why the mention in Galatians 1:21 appears in reverse order. Several factors could have accounted for this way of mention. Syria was the more prominent of the areas, and Paul could have merely used a common designation, as did Luke in Acts 15:41. He had no particular reason to preserve the chronological order in which he ministered there. The mention of Syria first could be a reflection of the importance of Paul's labors, for his ministry in Syrian Antioch seems to have eclipsed in importance his labors in Tarsus of Cilicia. Those who insist that the proper sequence must be preserved may argue that Paul's journey to Tarsus from Caesarea (Acts 9:30) could have been by land rather than by sea as is usually concluded, and this would have taken him through Syria first. Even if he went by sea, his ship could have touched at various Syrian ports before reaching Cilicia.

VERSE 22. During these approximately eleven years in Tarsus and Antioch, Paul had no contact at all with Jerusalem. He was becoming progressively unknown[18] by face to the Christian churches[19] of Judea.[20] His departure from Jerusalem had been abrupt, and had taken him directly to the port of Caesarea and then to Tarsus. Paul's statement argues against the idea that the next Jerusalem visit to be mentioned in Galatians (2:1-10) is the Jerusalem Council visit, for that would require that the Famine visit (Acts 11:29-30) occurred during this period when he said he was "unknown by face" in Judea.

VERSES 23-24. Paul's reputation, however, was spreading. Even those who did not know him personally or had never even seen him were continually hearing reports of the startling

---

[17]M. J. Mellink, "Cilicia," The Interpreter's Dictionary of the Bible, ed. G. A. Buttrick (New York, 1962), vol. A-D, p. 628; E. M. B. Green, "Cilicia," The New Bible Dictionary, ed. J. D. Douglas (Grand Rapids, 1962), p. 233.

[18]Greek: ēmēn de agnooumenos. The imperfect periphrastic form emphasizes the continuing progress of the condition.

[19]The plural ekklēsiais as compared to the singular ekklēsian in 1:13 is another evidence (cf. 1:2) that Paul had the concept of both a universal church and local churches.

[20]This reference to Judea could denote the area outside of Jerusalem. A similar usage occurs in John 3:22.

change in the former persecutor. The one who had once hounded Christians even to death (Acts 7:58; 8:1-3; 26:10) now was spreading the good news of the Christian faith. "The faith" seems here to be a synonym for the gospel, showing the importance of faith in the mind of the early church and its preachers. The fact that such reports were spreading during these years may indicate that Paul was not inactive while he was in Tarsus, although admittedly the time involved includes his presence in Antioch as well as Tarsus. Acts mentions nothing about his activities in Tarsus, and gives no indication that churches had been planted by him in Cilicia at this time; nevertheless it must not necessarily be concluded that Paul devoted these years solely to personal study and meditation. His continuing preaching which was reported in Judea could have involved Tarsus as well as Antioch. The result was that the churches "were glorifying God because of me" (NASB). Only God could have wrought the change in Paul, and the churches did not miss the point. How different from some of the Galatians' attitude was that of these former victims of the persecutor! They gave God, not Paul, the glory; but they certainly did not vilify Paul as some in Galatia were doing. What the Judean Christians were doing was to rejoice in God's action, and to regard Paul with the right perspective. Two extremes should be avoided. In a day when it is so common to glorify "ex-sinners," the church would do well to heed the example of these Judean brethren in giving God the glory. At the same time, there should be rejoicing in every new evidence of God's saving work among men, and those whom He transforms should be welcomed with joy as trophies of God's grace.

Paul has thus shown in this portion of his account that his message was not imparted to him by the apostles, by the Jerusalem church, or by other churches in Judea. Yet during all this time he had been preaching and his fame had been growing. Furthermore, there was no suspicion about the truth of his message by any of the churches. To charge, as some in Galatia were apparently doing, that Paul was both doctrinally unorthodox and also not a true apostle equal to the Twelve was to make accusations unsupported by the historical facts. His message, therefore, is not to be suspected. It was given to him by

Christ, and thus it speaks with as great an authority to us today as it did to the Galatian churches nineteen centuries ago.

Questions for Discussion

1. Why would the Judaizers wish to charge Paul with getting his gospel from men?
2. If the Judaizers thought that the Twelve supported their legalistic teaching, why would they say Paul got his gospel from them?
3. What was the function of Ananias in regard to Paul's conversion, in the light of Paul's claim that his gospel did not come from man?
4. Why was Paul so insistent that the sketch of his early activities was no lie?
5. Why did the early Christians refer to the gospel as "the faith"? Are there any implications here for twentieth-century Christians?
6. Was James the Lord's brother an apostle?

Chapter 3

Paul's Second Trip to Jerusalem

(Galatians 2:1-10)

As Paul defends himself and the gospel of grace which he preached, he has already shown that his enemies had no basis for claiming that he was really dependent on the Twelve in Jerusalem (cf. 1:11-24). Throughout the first fourteen years of his Christian life he had visited Jerusalem but once, and that was for only fifteen days during which he became acquainted with Peter and James but saw no other apostles. His opponents, however, were not likely to yield so easily. They must certainly have known that there had been later contacts between Paul and Jerusalem, and that the very points at issue (the relation of Gentile converts to the Mosaic requirements) had been discussed with some of the Twelve. Perhaps it had been implied by the Judaizers that at some such meeting Paul was made dependent upon those in Jerusalem. Hence Paul must show how it was still true that he was not subordinate to the other apostles, and yet that he and they were in essential agreement as to the content of the gospel.

C. Paul's Second Trip to Jerusalem (2:1-2)

1. *After fourteen years Paul went again to Jerusalem.* (2:1-2)

VERSE 1. "Then" (*epeita*) introduces what is apparently Paul's next visit to Jerusalem. In accordance with the data in Acts, this must refer to the trip made by Paul and Barnabas to deliver the famine relief from the church at Antioch (Acts 11:29-30; 12:25).[1]

---

[1]The alternate view equates Gal. 2:1-10 with the Jerusalem Council of Acts 15, but labors under the difficulty that Paul is assumed to have omitted mention of the Famine visit. Proponents usually explain that Paul did not mention it because he contacted no apostles on that occasion. However, in view of his obvious effort to be absolutely truthful and to answer all possible charges against him, it seems unlikely that he would have left one visit unmentioned, specially if he could have used it (as the proponents claim) to support his contention that he saw no one of importance. See Introduction ("Date") for discussion of the problem.

This trip came after an interval[2] of fourteen years[3] (see Fig. 4). It should be clear that Paul's contacts with any Jerusalem leaders had been few indeed.

Barnabas accompanied Paul on this visit to Jerusalem (cf. Acts 11:29-30). He was the man who first introduced Paul to the Jerusalem leaders, and who later had recruited him to assist in the growing church at Antioch (Acts 11:25-26). He also had an excellent reputation among those at Jerusalem. His stellar Christian character had caused him to be given the name "Son of encouragement," by which he has been known ever since (Acts 4:36). Of course, Barnabas was well known to the Galatian readers, for he and Paul had formed the missionary team which had recently brought the gospel to the regions of Galatia (Acts 13, 14).

On this trip to Jerusalem, Paul and Barnabas were accompanied by Titus. The way in which Titus is mentioned indicates that he was taken along in a somewhat subordinate capacity.[4] Titus is not mentioned in the Book of Acts in connection with this visit (or any other). Perhaps it was because the main purpose of the trip involved another matter, and the episode with Titus did not loom that large in Luke's historical perspective. As Paul, however, argues for the purity of the gospel, the incident of Titus provided an illustration to support his case.

VERSE 2. This second visit to Jerusalem was made "in accord with revelation" (kata apokalupsin). Assuming that the Famine visit is meant, the reference is probably to the prophecy of Agabus, who predicted by the Spirit the coming famine which would bring such hardship to the believers in Judea (Acts

---

[2]The use of dia with the accusative to denote an interval occurs also in Mark 2:1 and Acts 24:17.

[3]The mention of fourteen years does not determine whether the Famine visit or the Jerusalem Council is in view because the chronology can be adjusted to fit either scheme. If the Famine visit is meant, the years must be computed from Paul's conversion (not from his last-mentioned visit). If the Jerusalem Council is in view, then Paul means fourteen years after the first visit (1:18).

[4]The other NT uses of sumparalambanō (take along with) support this conclusion (Acts 12:25; 15:37, 38). This agrees with the Famine visit account where Paul and Barnabas were apparently the only two officially chosen by the church. At the Jerusalem Council, however, the Antioch church officially sent "certain others" (tinas allous) as equal delegates with Paul and Barnabas (Acts 15:2).

11:27-28). In response to that divinely revealed information, Paul and Barnabas were sent to Jerusalem with relief funds or provisions for the church.

While they were in Jerusalem, Paul took advantage of the opportunity to discuss privately with the leaders certain features regarding his ministry and message. "Communicated" (anethemēn) means to "lay before someone for consideration."[5] There were many Gentiles in the church at Antioch (Acts 11:20-21), and Paul's ministry there may have caused questions to arise at Jerusalem, just as did the case of Peter and his relations with the house of Cornelius some time before (Acts 11:1-18). What Paul did, therefore, was to lay before the leaders at Jerusalem the very issue that the Judaizers were agitating—should Gentiles be compelled to adopt circumcision and other Mosaic rites in order to be Christians? Paul had been preaching that such was not the case. He wanted to be sure that the Jerusalem leaders understood his position, and that he could count on their support.

"Those which were of reputation" utilizes an expression occurring four times in this passage.[6] It is used in its common meaning of "seem" in 2:6a ("those who seem to be something") and 2:9 ("those who seem to be pillars"), but appears alone in 2:2 and 2:6b with an apparent idiomatic or technical sense, "the ones of reputation" or "those who seem to be the leaders." From 2:9 it is clear that the references are to James, Cephas (Peter), and John. Paul can hardly be speaking of them in a disparaging sense, for this would not have helped his argument (he was showing that they were in complete agreement as equals). If there is any shadow cast by the repeated use of this terminology, it may be because Paul has adopted the slogans of his opponents who had claimed (erroneously) the support of these "pillars" from Jerusalem.

The reason why Paul approached these leaders regarding his message is explained as "lest by any means I should run, or had run, in vain." This clause may be understood in several ways. One way is to regard it as an object clause after a verb of fearing

---

[6]Tois dokousin (2:2); tōn dokountōn einai ti (2:6a); hoi dokountes (2:6b); hoi dokountes stuloi einai (2:9).

[5]Arndt, p. 61.

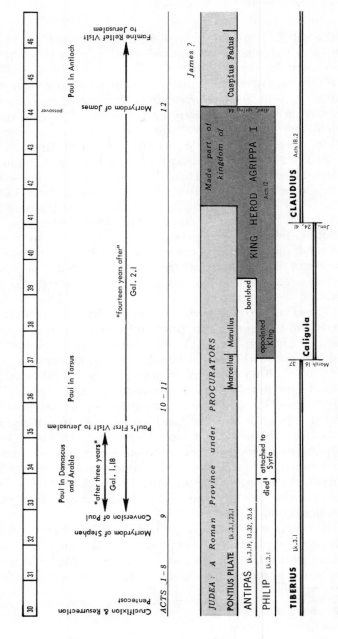

Fig. 4. Time Chart I: A.D. 30-46.

understood: "[fearing] lest I may be running, or did run, in vain."[7] Of course, Paul was not fearful that his gospel was wrong, for he has just stated that he got it by direct revelation from Christ. His fear may have been that if he were undercut by those at Jerusalem, his ministry among Gentiles would be greatly hampered, and churches already established among Gentiles might even be wrecked by Judaizing influences. Another possibility is to treat the clause as an indirect question: "[asking them] whether I am running, or did run, in vain."[8] Such a question would not necessarily express a doubt on Paul's part, but would merely be asking the Jerusalem leaders to confirm his own position publicly in the face of Judaizing detractors who had first raised the question. The answer Paul expected to such a question was an emphatic "No, you are not running in vain."

2. Titus was a test case for circumcision requirements. (2:3-5)

VERSES 3-4. The episode with Titus is not mentioned in Acts, but it provided an excellent illustration for Paul's present purpose to show the nature of the issue and to demonstrate the official attitude of the church in relation to Paul's policy. "But not even Titus,"[9] he says, "although he was a Greek, was compelled to be circumcised." It is not absolutely certain where this incident occurred, but the simplest reading of the text leads one to conclude that it happened on this visit to Jerusalem. (Pressure for it, however, could have begun earlier at Antioch, and the issue then came to a climax at Jerusalem.) The Judaizers wanted to force circumcision on all Gentile converts, but not only were they unsuccessful in that broad aim, but "not even Titus" could be forced to submit to that rite, even though he was present at Jerusalem with Paul and thus presented a most obvious opportunity for an attempt to be made. Titus was a pure

---

[7]This construction requires the first verb trechō to be regarded as subjunctive, rather than indicative, and is the more common construction with mē pōs.

[8]If the clause is an indirect question, both verbs would be indicative.

[9]Greek: all' oude Titos.

Gentile,[10] not partly Jewish as Timothy (Acts 16:1), and Paul regarded any yielding to suggestions that Titus be circumcised to be a sacrifice of principle.

The use of the strong verb "compelled" (ēnangkasthē) indicates the pressure put on Titus to submit to this Jewish rite. The pressure came not from "those of reputation" (2:2), but from certain "false brethren" (2:4).[11] Paul regards them as not even true Christians, but ones who were somehow smuggled into the church, presumably at Jerusalem. He does not indicate who smuggled them in, and the active voice of the verb "came in" (pareisēlthon) makes it clear that the false brethren themselves were active agents in the episode, not merely passive tools of someone else. They must have appeared to be orthodox Jewish Christians, but their true colors came to light when the issue of Gentile salvation was confronted. They had no conception of salvation except on the basis of performing works of law. They viewed with complete antipathy any extension of the gospel to Gentiles as such, apart from compelling them to become full proselytes to Judaism. Thus the "liberty" which is offered in Christ was regarded as enemy territory to them, something "to spy out"[12] and ultimately to capture and enslave. Perhaps they had joined the Christian community with the express purpose of setting things right according to their traditional understanding.

VERSE 5. For these false Christians to have succeeded would have meant that all true Christians would be enslaved. Gentile converts would have been forced to observe Mosaic ceremonies against their will, and Jewish Christians also would have been given the false impression that righteousness is obtained by works of law. Therefore, Paul, Barnabas, and Titus would not

---

[10]The description of him as Hellēn (Greek) is probably in the broad sense of Gentile, or one who was under the influence of Greek culture, in contrast to a Jew. The expression Ioudaioi kai Hellēnes (Jews and Greeks) covers the entire human race (3:28; Col. 3:11).

[11]I understand the syntactical difficulties of 2:4 to be eased by ignoring the editors' punctuation at the close of 2:3, and attaching 2:4 to what precedes. The postpositive de is understood here as the intensive "even." Thus, "But not even Titus . . . was compelled to be circumcised, even on account of the false brethren. . . ."

[12]The verb kataskopeō is used of spies in Josh. 2:1-3 and II Sam. 10:3 (LXX).

yield, "not even for a moment."[13] To have done so might have eased the pressure at the moment, but would have been disastrous for the future. It would have undermined the "truth of the gospel" which had been so carefully and courageously presented to the Galatians on the recent journey. Paul was not unmindful of the need to protect the sensitivities of weaker brethren, and he was always willing to forego his personal liberties in order to win others (Rom. 14:21; 15:1; I Cor. 8:13; 9:19-20). It would not help anyone, however, if momentary expediency were allowed to violate principle, and cause the very heart of the gospel of God's grace to be lost in the process. Paul could draw fine distinctions. On another occasion[14] he approved the circumcision of Timothy because he was partly Jewish, and the operation served to regularize his status and make possible a ministry for him in Jewish synagogues (Acts 16:3). There the principle of salvation was not at stake, for it was not done to placate Jewish Christians but to gain access to unsaved Jews in their synagogues. The issue in Jerusalem, however, was the theological one of the nature of the gospel. Paul knew that the truth of the gospel is the proclamation that salvation is available to all men solely on the merits of Christ, and this message would be shattered by the restrictions that the Judaizers were proposing.

Paul's dramatic battle for the truth should remind all Christians of the constant threat which faces the gospel. Man has always tried to devise schemes whereby human efforts make some contribution to win the favorable verdict of God. The truth of the gospel declares that man is powerless to save himself. Man's best efforts at righteousness fall short of the perfection which God requires (Jas. 2:10). Salvation must be recognized as the free and loving gift of God, granted to men who will accept it solely on the merits of Christ who died for sinners.

---

[13]Greek: *hois oude pros hōran*. The words *hois oude* (to whom not even) are omitted in the Western text, thus supporting the view that Paul did yield for a moment. Manuscript evidence, however, is decidedly in favor of retaining the words, and the tenor of the passage makes it most unlikely that Titus was actually circumcised.

[14]The date of Galatians assumed here places the Timothy incident subsequent to the episode with Titus. Those who date Galatians later regard the circumcision of Timothy as having occurred previously. (See Introduction, "Date.")

3. *The leaders at Jerusalem contributed nothing to Paul's gospel.* (2:6-10)

VERSE 6. After the brief mention of the case of Titus, Paul resumes the discussion of 2:1-2. He picks up the phrase *tois dokousin* ("the ones of reputation," 2:2), and says, "But from those reputed to be something" (*apo de tōn dokountōn einai ti*). Before he finishes his sentence, he pauses to make a parenthetical comment which probably reflects some of the Judaizers' claims that were meant to downgrade Paul. "What sort they were formerly makes no difference to me." The key to Paul's thought is the past tense "were" (*ēsan*) and the adverbial particle which means "formerly" when used with past time verbs. Hence he refers to the previous experiences of James, Peter, and John, which must have been cited by the Judaizers as making them vastly superior to Paul. James was the Lord's brother (1:19) who had obviously known Jesus intimately. The other two were part of the Twelve, and had been with Jesus for three years in the closest of personal associations.

Now Paul was not disparaging these "pillars." At the most, all he was doing was questioning the extravagant and erroneous claims made for them by the Judaizers. He himself was happy to claim their friendship and support (2:9), and he would have defeated his own purposes if he conveyed the idea that the leaders at Jerusalem were of no account. His point was that their human experiences were not the issue. What matters is the source of their apostolic authority. If it came from God (and, of course, Paul understood that it did), then it should be remembered that God doesn't choose men on the basis of outward circumstances and reputation (I Sam. 16:7). What constitutes someone an apostle is the appointment by Christ, and it had been amply demonstrated in the case of Paul by the Damascus road experience and subsequent events that his appointment as an apostle had been as directly the act of Christ as theirs had been.

Following the parenthetical explanation, the thought is resumed even though the sentence structure is somewhat broken.[15] These leaders in Jerusalem contributed nothing to him regarding his gospel. The verb *prosanatithēmi* occurs only here and in 1:16 in the New Testament. The cognate *anatithēmi* was used in 2:2. The word means to confer with and expound something to someone for consideration and decision.[16] In 1:16 Paul has said he did not originally confer with any human being regarding his message. In 2:2 he did go to Jerusalem and conveyed to certain ones there an explanation of what he was doing so that they might understand and concur in what he was doing. On the other hand, in 2:6 he says that the leaders did not place anything before him for consideration and adoption regarding the gospel. Thus they recognized that Paul's preaching had no lack in its content. He was not beholden to them in any way for his authority or message.

VERSES 7-8. The leaders at Jerusalem, rather than modifying or contributing anything to Paul, simply recognized that different spheres of ministry had been entrusted to Paul and Peter. "The gospel of the uncircumcision" is not a different gospel from that "of the circumcision." Paul has already made it clear in the epistle that there is only one gospel (1:8-9). The consultation among the leaders did recognize, however, that Paul had been particularly entrusted by God with preaching the gospel to uncircumcised Gentiles. It is not revealed how they came to this recognition. Most likely it was a conclusion drawn from the evidence of Paul's conversion and commission (Acts 9:15), coupled with God's blessing on his subsequent preaching ministry among Gentiles (Acts 11:26). These spheres of ministry were not ironclad separations, for Paul regularly preached first in synagogues whenever he visited new areas (both Gentiles and Jews were named in his commission, Acts 9:15), and Peter preached to Gentiles as well as Jews (e.g., Cornelius, Acts 10). Nor should it be supposed that these areas were arbitrarily assigned at some apostolic meeting. Paul makes it clear that "he

---

[15]The sentence would have been expected to continue with a first person subject and a verb, such as: "I received nothing." However, Paul takes the object of the prepositional phrase "those who seemed," repeats it, and makes it the subject of a verb: "those who seemed added nothing."

[16]J. Behm, "Anatithēmi, Prosanatithēmi," *TDNT*, 1, 353-54.

who effectually worked for Peter . . . effectually worked for me also" (NASB), and the reference is obviously to God. It was God who had appointed both Peter and Paul to the apostleship, and had made them effective in these general areas. They were not rivals, nor was one subordinate to the other. Both spheres of ministry were God-given and were recognized as such by Paul and those at Jerusalem.

VERSE 9. Having understood[17] the divine gift of grace which had been given to Paul (i.e., his apostolic appointment), James, Cephas, and John—the ones referred to earlier in a veiled way as "those of reputation"—are here identified and are shown to have concurred fully in Paul's message and ministry. These leaders gave to Paul and Barnabas "right hands of fellowship." The right hand (hē dexia) was a commonly used symbol of friendship or trust, often employed in finalizing a treaty or compact.[18] The first century Jewish historian Josephus used the same expression regarding the Roman general (later emperor) Vespasian, who he said "sent immediately and zealously two tribunes, Paulinus and Gallicanus, and ordered them to give Josephus their right hands as a security for his life, and to order him to come up."[19] Lest the readers mistakenly suppose that these "right hands" or pledges involved some sort of submission on his part or an authorization from the leaders, Paul specified that they were "right hands of fellowship." It was a mutual recognition of a common enterprise. Within the framework of this common goal it was understood that Paul and Barnabas would be laboring primarily in Gentile territories, whereas James, Cephas, and John were, at least at that time, ministering chiefly in geographical areas where Jews were predominant.

The James mentioned here is the brother of the Lord, named earlier in 1:19. If it is wondered why he is not so identified in 2:9 to distinguish him from the James who was one of the Twelve,

---

[17]The participle gnontes (2:9) is parallel to idontes (2:7), and the difference may be only literary. If different concepts are meant, idontes (having seen) could refer to outward apprehension of the evidences of Paul's distinctive sphere of ministry, and gnontes (having known) could denote the inward recognition and understanding (so Lightfoot, Galatians, p. 109).

[18]Arndt, p. 173; W. Grundmann, "Dexios," TDNT, 2, 38.

[19]Josephus The Jewish War 3, 344 (3. 8. 1).

Fig. 5. Jerusalem, where Paul met with the church and its leaders. *Kent*

the answer is probably that such an identification was necessary at the time of Paul's first visit to Jerusalem (1:18-19) because both Jameses were then alive. However, by the time of Paul's second visit (A.D. 46), the apostle James had already been killed, so that James the brother of the Lord would have been the only prominent James left at Jerusalem (see Fig. 4). This James came increasingly to the forefront in the Jerusalem church as the resident leader after the Twelve undertook their extensive journeys (see Acts 12:17; 21:18). Perhaps this also explains why he is mentioned first among the three, ahead of the two apostles.

The Aramaic name Cephas is used in 2:9, perhaps because that was the way Peter was commonly referred to at Jerusalem among his associates where these events occurred (so also 1:18). The apostle John exercised some of his earliest ministry in close association with Peter (Acts 3:1, 3, 11: 4:13; 8:14, 25). These two were presumably the only apostles in Jerusalem on this occasion.

VERSE 10. The only exception to the principle that Paul and Barnabas would concentrate on the Gentiles was that they should continue remembering the poor. Presumably this refers to the plight of the poor saints at Jerusalem, whose condition was a lingering one, made more acute in times of persecution. On the assumption that this action occurred at the Famine visit, the plea is specially meaningful. One generous gift from Antioch which had just been brought (Acts 11:29-30), although deeply appreciated, would by no means have permanently alleviated their distress. Hence Paul was urged to make the poor a matter of continuing concern among the Gentile churches. "Which very thing," said Paul, "I also made every effort[20] to do." Paul did maintain throughout his ministry a strong interest in the poor Jerusalem saints, and undertook active measures to care for their physical needs (Acts 24:17; Rom. 15:25-27; I Cor. 16:1-4; II Cor. 8-9).

Paul has thus shown that when he finally had contact with the Twelve and others at Jerusalem, and when they actually did discuss the content of the gospel which he preached, two things were crystal clear. He was not subordinate to the pillars at Jerusalem; neither were they in disagreement. He made a clear presentation of his gospel to them so they could examine it, but they laid nothing before him for the purpose of instructing him. Hence the result was a clearly indicated agreement, with right hands clasped in fellowship and mutual commitment. Those in Galatia who were trying to drive a wedge between Paul and the Twelve at Jerusalem were either misinformed or wilfully malicious.

Questions for Discussion

1. What was Paul's reason for conferring with the leaders at Jerusalem about the gospel?
2. Why did Paul refuse to allow the circumcision of Titus but authorize the rite for Timothy?

---

[20]The aorist verb *espoudasa* is probably ingressive, denoting the beginning of an action that Paul actually pursued during much of his subsequent ministry. F. F. Bruce, however, suggests that the aorist here may have pluperfect force, and thus may refer to what he had already done ("Galatian Problems. 1. Autobiographical Data," *Bulletin of the John Rylands Library*, vol. 51, no. 2 [Spring 1969], p. 305).

3. How does one decide in cases of Christian disagreement whether to yield a point so as not to give offense, or to stand firm at all costs?
4. Which of the men named James in the New Testament is referred to in 2:9? How do we know?
5. What are the Biblical guidelines regarding Christian concern for those in economic need?

Chapter 4

Peter and Paul at Antioch

(Galatians 2:11-21)

The clash between Peter and Paul at Antioch must surely rank as one of the most intriguing episodes in New Testament history. These two dynamic leaders among Christ's apostles are in face-to-face confrontation, and one of them boldly rebukes the other in the presence of the whole church! The reader immediately desires to learn more about this fascinating incident, but when he searches for additional details, he finds nothing. No mention of this encounter occurs in the Book of Acts. Neither Peter in his epistles nor Paul in any of his other writings makes the slightest reference to this traumatic meeting in Antioch. All of our knowledge must be gained from this one passage in Galatians. So puzzling is this episode, and so embarrassing is it to extravagant views on the infallibility of the apostles that some early interpreters explained this "Cephas" as being another person, one of the seventy perhaps,[1] or else as a maneuver contrived among the apostles who both held the same view but used this device to condemn Judaizers by apparently discrediting Peter whom the Judaizers kept quoting.[2] No warrant exists, however, for any such treatment of the passage.

Fascinating as the incident is, it must have been quickly settled and thus offered no lasting problems to the church. It was the sort of problem that can occur when some of the ramifications of an action are seen by one party but not the other. To expand this brief conflict into a continuing battle between Peter and Paul and their respective supporters is without sufficient basis in the New Testament record.

[1]Quoted from Clement's *Hypotyposes*, book 5 (no longer extant) by Eusebius *Ecclesiastical History* 1. 12. *The Fathers of the Church: Eusebius Pamphili*, books 1-5, trans. Roy J. Deferrari (Washington, D.C., 1953), p. 75.
[2]This view was espoused by Jerome in his commentary on Galatians, and was argued in a series of letters with Augustine. *St. Jerome: Letters and Select Works*, trans. W. H. Fremantle, in *The Nicene and Post-Nicene Fathers* (Grand Rapids, repr.), 6, 112.

Fig. 6. Site of Syrian Antioch. Mount Silpius is at right. *Levant*

In the course of Paul's defending of himself against the challenge to his authority by some in Galatia, he has shown that his apostolic appointment came directly from Jesus Christ (1:12). He then demonstrated that even though he was independent of the Twelve, he was in basic agreement with them, and his gospel had their full endorsement (2:6-10). The climax of this defense is reached when Paul shows how he actually rebuked Peter on one occasion and was instrumental in calling him back to the true principle of Christian conduct which the gospel sets forth. Thus Paul shows himself to be no innovator, nor inferior to the Twelve; but actually in this instance he took a position superior to Peter by publicly censuring him, giving a rebuke which Peter apparently accepted with good grace. This description of the clash with Peter not only pointed out Paul's authority as being equal to any possessed by the Twelve, but the issue involved was related to that which was troubling the Galatians, and was thus of particular appropriateness in this letter.

D. Paul's Encounter with Peter at Antioch (2:11-21)

1. The episode described. (2:11-14)

VERSE 11. At some time in the past, Peter[3] had come to Antioch and in Paul's view had acted in a blameworthy manner. Inasmuch as there is no other New Testament mention of this visit, it is difficult to know when it occurred. Because Paul has been listing events in chronological sequence throughout his discussion (cf. 1:18; 2:1), presumably 2:11-21 occurred following the visit to Jerusalem described in 2:1-10.[4] The assumption adopted here is that 2:1-10 refers to the Famine visit. Hence a time must be found when Paul, Peter, and Barnabas were all present in Antioch. Although Peter is not mentioned in Acts as being in Antioch, Paul and Barnabas were there together before the first missionary journey (Acts 13:1) and for a considerable time after their return (Acts 14:26-28). Hence Peter's visit could have occurred during either of those periods.

Paul opposed Peter to his face because of what was happening. "Opposed" (antestēn) means literally "to stand against," and implies a response made to an attack, whether through offering firm resistance or by opposing with some counter measures. His statement indicates that Peter's action was really an attack on the principle which the gospel supports, even if Peter was not conscious of it. Paul opposed Peter "because he stood condemned" (NASB). He did not mean that Peter had been condemned by any sort of official action in Antioch,[5] but that by his own inconsistent action he had rendered himself guilty.[6]

---

[3]In the Greek text Peter is called by his Aramaic name Kēphas throughout this passage.

[4]Admittedly there is no reason why this must be so, but it is assumed as most probable unless it can be shown that other factors make it unlikely.

[5]K. S. Wuest, however, states: "He stood condemned by the Christians of Antioch. The public judgment had turned against him." Galatians in the Greek New Testament (Grand Rapids, 1944, p. 70).

[6]The pluperfect periphrastic kategnōsmenos ēn may be regarded as a middle, rather than passive; hence, "he had condemned himself." In this instance, however, the difference in sense would be slight inasmuch as the passive would infer the same thing.

VERSE 12. Previously Peter had been eating regularly[7] with the Gentile Christians at Antioch. The passage requires some sort of common meals in which both Jewish and Gentile believers participated. Conceivably the Antioch church could have practiced a community of goods as did the Jerusalem church, or at least have provided regular meals for its full-time leaders.[8] It is more likely, however, that the problem arose at the love feasts at which the communion elements of the bread and the cup were also partaken.[9] At Antioch no issue had ever been raised as to whether Jews and Gentiles should or should not eat together, and therefore they had always done so, Peter included.

When "certain men from James" arrived, Peter gradually left the side of his Gentile friends. Who these men were is not stated beyond this. It is not said that they "came" from James, as though James had authorized their coming.[10] Hence it is better to understand the statement as meaning simply that they came from the Jerusalem church where James was the resident leader. Some have suggested that they were the same as the "certain men from Judea" (Acts 15:1) whose action at Antioch precipitated the Jerusalem Council.[11] It is possible, of course, that the episode occurred before the first missionary journey. If they were the same as those mentioned in Acts 15:1, the Jerusalem church specifically disavowed granting them any authorization (Acts 15:24).

This Jewish contingent from Jerusalem had extremely conservative views of the conduct expected of Christian Jews. They ate only kosher foods at home and saw no reason to vary the practice when they visited Antioch. One can imagine that they strongly disapproved (albeit silently) of any Jew who did not do likewise. Peter was well aware of their feelings, and he knew how conspicuous he must have been to the Jerusalem visitors as he ate freely with the Gentile believers in Antioch. Consequently, he

---

[7]The imperfect tense of *sunesthien* (was eating) describes his habitual activity. It also implies that Peter had been in Antioch for some time.

[8]R. A. Cole, *The Epistle of Paul to the Galatians* (Grand Rapids, 1965), p. 74.

[9]See I Cor. 11:18-34 for another instance in a Gentile Church of fellowship meals at which the communion elements of the bread and the cup were utilized.

[10]The Greek expression *elthein tinas apo Iakobou* seems to construe "from James" with the subject "certain men," rather than with the verbal idea.

[11]F. F. Bruce, *The Book of the Acts* (Grand Rapids, 1954), p. 303.

embarked on a course of action that was prompted not by principle but by fear in the presence of those who stressed circumcision and other Jewish practices. He gradually withdrew[12] and separated himself from the Gentiles, until eventually he was associating exclusively with the Jews from Jerusalem.

VERSE 13. The break was not abrupt but gradual; nevertheless its significance was not missed by the others. The other Jewish Christians at Antioch quickly followed his example. Even Barnabas, who had been such an early supporter of Gentile evangelism (Acts 11:22-26), joined this unseemly migration.

Paul says their action was "hypocrisy."[13] It was not merely inconsistent but hypocritical because they all knew better. Peter fully understood that Jewish regulations were not mandatory for any Christian. He knew that it was not right to impose these practices on Gentiles, and he also knew that no Jewish Christian was required to observe them either. He had eaten with Gentiles at the house of Cornelius and had defended his action before the Jerusalem church (Acts 11:2-3). He had been doing the same thing at Antioch. By abandoning the Gentile Christians when the Jerusalem group arrived, he was acting in a way that did not properly represent what he really believed. It was, said Paul, hypocrisy pure and simple.

VERSE 14. When Paul saw that the shift in conduct on the part of Peter and the others was not straightforward in regard to the truth of the gospel which says that all believers in Christ are constituted a spiritual unity without such earthly distinctions (3:28), he addressed Peter publicly on the subject. If it is thought that Paul should have been more diplomatic and have talked privately to Peter, it should be remembered that Peter's duplicity had been done in public and was having public consequences. Apparently Paul felt the issue needed prompt and public clarification lest whispering campaigns begin and confusion reign. The question he put left the answer up to Peter. He was allowing the circumstances to speak for themselves. The question may be paraphrased as follows: If you, Peter, while being a Jew by descent, normally live like the Christian Gentiles here at An-

---

[12]The verbs *hupestellen* and *aphōrizen* are both imperfects, showing the action as gradual and not done all at once.

[13]Greek: *sunupekrithēsan, hupokrisei* (v. 13).

tioch and have not been scrupulously observing all the kosher
practices of Jewish tradition until the visitors from Jerusalem
arrived, how can you now defend your action of compelling the
Gentile Christians to live according to Jewish customs? Peter, of
course, had not at all been teaching the Gentiles to adopt Jewish
regulations, but his action in changing groups was a clear
proclamation that Jewish practices were preferable. Hence those
who looked to Peter for leadership as an apostle could not avoid
feeling the compulsion of his example. Apparently the Jewish
Christians followed at once (2:13). The Gentile Christians must
certainly have been thrown into consternation.

2. The principle involved. (2:15-21)

Whether the verses which follow are a continuation of Paul's
remarks to Peter, or are an elaboration of the principle and are
addressed primarily to the Galatians, cannot be determined with
certainty. The interpretation is not affected, for in either case the
words are an explanation of the principle which applied to both
Peter and the Galatians.

VERSES 15-16. Paul first makes the point that even Jewish
Christians must depend on Christ alone for justification
(2:15-16). "We Jews by nature" means those like Paul and Peter
who were Jews by descent as well as by religion. "Sinners from
among the Gentiles" was an expression reflecting a Jewish
viewpoint, in which "sinners" (hamartōlōi) was virtually a
synonym for "Gentiles."[14] Paul may have used it with a bit of
irony, remembering how the more scrupulous Jews may have
referred to the Gentile converts. Even Jewish Christians knew
that a man was not declared righteous by the verdict of God as a
consequence of performing works of law (ex ergōn nomou), but
rather[15] through faith in Jesus Christ.[16] Thus every true Jewish

---

[14]Compare Matt. 26:45 (sinners) and Mark 14:41 (sinners) with Luke 18:32
(Gentiles), and Luke 6:32 (sinners) with Matt. 5:47 (Gentiles, NASB).

[15]This use of ean mē (except, but) is not exceptive but adversative, one of its
common functions in the NT. Compare the similar use of ei mē in 1:19.

[16]The genitive Iēsou Christou after pisteōs should be understood as objective:
"faith in Jesus Christ."

Christian had trusted Christ for his justification. Peter understood this and used the same argument himself at the Jerusalem
Council soon after (Acts 15:10-11).

Justification refers to the act of God in which He deals with the
sinner who trusts in Christ and pronounces him righteous. Personal transformation of life (i.e., sanctification) is not in view at
this point, but one's standing before the judgment bar of God. On
the merits of Christ, whose blood satisfied God's broken law,
righteousness is imputed to the sinner by faith, and the believer
is declared by God as acquitted of all guilt and all possibility of
condemnation. To Paul there was no other way for a sinner to
achieve righteousness in God's eyes. Unless God should freely
offer it through Christ, man must achieve it himself through
compliance with God's laws. Yet the very Scriptures which the
Judaizers professed to be upholding indicated that "as a consequence of works of law no flesh shall be justified."[17] Justification in Christ is man's only hope.

VERSE 17. Paul develops the thought by asking a question. If
the Christian practice of looking to Christ alone for justification
makes such believers no better than "sinners of the Gentiles,"
then is Christ the minister of sin (inasmuch as following Christ is
what causes Christians to forsake the law)? To this Paul gives a
resounding no! Such a conclusion is utterly unthinkable (*mē
genoito*).

"While seeking to be justified by Christ" (*zētountes
dikaiōthēnai en Christōi*) is not limited to the act of conversion,
but describes the continued experience of Christians. Believers
are persons who not only exercised faith in Christ initially but
who continue to believe (hence they are called "believers").

The remainder of 2:17 has been interpreted many ways.[18]
Although it is often explained as a Pauline answer to charges
that trusting Christ alone without the requirements of the law

---

[17]The language is an allusion to Ps. 143:2.

[18]An excellent résumé is given by E. D. Burton, *The Epistle to the Galatians*
(Edinburgh, 1921), pp. 127-30. See also J. B. Lightfoot, *The Epistle of St. Paul to
the Galatians* (Grand Rapids, reprint ed.), pp. 116-17; W. Hendriksen,
Exposition of Galatians (Grand Rapids, 1968), pp. 99-100.

leads to lawless conduct,[19] this is not really the point of the context. Another common explanation sees "sinners" and "sin" here in their usual sense as unrighteous conduct, and interprets the passage as meaning both Jews and Gentiles are unmasked by Christ as being on a common plane as sinners.[20] But this explanation finds difficulty with the next statement, for having one's guilt as a sinner laid bare by Christ hardly lays Christ open to the charge of being a promoter of sin as the words imply. It is best, therefore, to regard Paul as using the word "sinners" (hamartōloi) in a sense that has been colored by the Jewish expression "sinners of the Gentiles" (ex ethnōn hamartōloi) in 2:15. His question means this: If Jews who believe in Christ for their justification then proceed to forsake their traditional adherence to all the rules of the Mosaic Law and begin living apart from it as did the Gentiles (and Jewish Christians in Antioch, including Peter, had been doing this), was this actually a sin against God, and one which Christ had prompted them to commit?[21] To Paul such a thought was monstrous, and he proceeds to show that it was the reverting to law which involved transgression, not the opposite.

VERSE 18. Paul uses himself as an illustration: "if I build again these things which I tore down"; but he really had Peter in mind, for this is what Peter was doing. The old distinctions between Jewish kosher eating and Gentile practices had been broken down by Peter, not only in the original experience with Cornelius but more recently in Antioch. Now he and Barnabas and the other Christian Jews at Antioch were reconstructing the old fences. They were saying by their actions that it did make a difference at whose table they ate. By so doing, says Paul, they were clearly acknowledging that their former practice was wrong. It was the same as saying that their earlier relaxing of Jewish food laws was a transgression of Mosaic Law for which God was holding them accountable, and now they were attempting to correct the situation.

---

[19]Frederic Rendall, "The Epistle to the Galatians" in The Expositor's Greek Testament (Grand Rapids, repr.), 3, 165.

[20]Marvin R. Vincent, Word Studies in the New Testament (Grand Rapids, 1946), 4, 105.

[21]This seems also to be the view of Hendriksen, Galatians, p. 100, and Lightfoot, Galatians, pp. 116-17.

VERSE 19. To reinstate the law was no solution, for Paul recognized that the law condemned him, and only identification with Christ could provide him with righteousness (2:19-21). The law demanded death for sin; it offered no hope of righteousness for sinners. Yet it was the very application of the law to him that ultimately set him free from the law. "Through the Law I died to the Law" (2:19, NASB). The death which the law of Moses demanded was accomplished by Christ. Because Paul by faith was now "in Christ," that is, identified with Him, the law's penalty has been exacted and the law is satisfied. It has no further claim on Paul or any other believer. By this life-sharing union with Christ, Paul was free to live unto God, no longer under condemnation.

VERSE 20. Verse 20 gives an elaboration of verse 19, and provides a concise statement of the very heart of the believer's new condition. He has died so far as the law is concerned because he has been crucified with Christ. The verb "crucified with" (sustauroō) is used literally of the robbers who were affixed to crosses alongside Jesus (Matt. 27:44; Mark 15:32; John 19:32). The only other New Testament occurrences are by Paul (Rom. 6:6; Gal. 2:20), where the meaning is figurative, describing the identification of the believer with Christ in the theological aspects of His crucifixion. The tense of the verb here is perfect (sunestaurōmai), which looks at an action that occurred in the past but which produced effects that still continue. When Christ was crucified, God identified every believer with His Son, and thus believers were crucified with Him. That crucifixion satisfied the penalty that God's broken law demanded, and its effects have never changed. The tense of the verb really implies "I was crucified with Christ and still am." Thus the accusing finger of the law cannot any longer point with condemnation against the person who is identified with Christ, for the full penalty has already been paid. Other references to the believer's identification with Christ in His death can be found in Romans 6:3-8 and Colossians 2:20; 3:3.

"And it is no longer I who live"[22] is Paul's assertion of the

---

[22]This translation of NASB of the clause zō de ouketi egō is decidedly preferable to the KJV, "nevertheless I live; yet not I." There is no clear reason for making two clauses from these words which contain only one verb and a subject

radical change brought about by regeneration. Clearly he is not teaching some sort of pantheistic absorption into deity whereby he no longer has any separate and conscious identity (for the rest of the verse uses "I live" twice). But he is insisting that the regeneration brought about by his identification with Christ involved a new life resulting from Christ living in him. "Christ liveth in me" is the distinctive mark of the saved person. Paul is explaining the difference between what he now is as a Christian and what he was previously as a tradition-oriented Jew without the real knowledge of God. It was not a reformation of his old sinful self, but the impartation of God's life. Here the emphasis is on Christ as dwelling in the believer. In the Upper Room Discourse by Jesus, He told the disciples that both He and the Father (John 14:23) as well as the Holy Spirit (John 14:16-17) would indwell believers. Hence the Christian has the Triune God within him to enable him to live a life of righteousness.

The identification of the believer with Christ is true not only regarding His crucifixion but also of the resurrection life which followed Christ's crucifixion (cf. Rom. 6:4-23; Col. 3:1-3). Even before the resurrection of physical bodies from the grave at Christ's return, believers have the privilege of pursuing their Christian lives ("in the flesh" here means temporal life) by relying on the Christ who died for them. Here Paul is talking about sanctification, the growth in holiness which is the responsibility of every person who has been declared righteous (i.e., justified) in Christ. Not only is justification received by faith, but sanctification also is accomplished by continuing faith in the Son of God. Holiness is not achieved by performing works of law, but by trusting solely in Christ, both as to the merits of His death on man's behalf and the continual guidance which His indwelling presence provides.

VERSE 21. By this principle, says Paul, "I do not nullify the grace of God" (NASB), in spite of what his opponents were probably alleging. But to reinstitute a system of human effort would do this very thing. Paul had seen the truth that salvation comes only by accepting God's grace as provided in Christ. If

pronoun which agrees with that verb. Furthermore, the KJV rendering has produced two contradictory clauses, requiring the insertion of "yet" for which there is no warrant in the Greek text.

one could obtain true righteousness (God's approval) by fulfilling the law, then Christ died needlessly. This was the unfortunate dilemma in which Peter's compromising conduct had placed him. Reverting to legal observances, and by implication asserting that they were valid for spiritual reasons, was to say that righteousness in some measure did come by the law.

Peter apparently corrected this error of conduct, inasmuch as we hear no more of it. It is a compliment to his Christian character that he bore Paul no ill-will as they continued to serve Christ as faithful apostles (II Peter 3:15). The incident is a reminder, however, that the principle of salvation by grace alone, apart from human merit of any kind, is too important to compromise. Historically, Paul used the encounter to show his Galatian converts that it was he who had continually proclaimed the true gospel, and not the Judaizers who may have tried to claim Peter (without his knowledge) as supporting their cause. The church should ever be grateful that Paul had the spiritual insight along with sufficient courage to set the record straight and to defend the grace of God against any who would dilute the gospel, whether by word or by conduct.

Questions for Discussion

1. What was wrong with Peter's conduct at Antioch?
2. Should a church ever refuse another Christian the privilege of eating the Lord's Supper?
3. Should a Christian ever refuse to eat the Lord's Supper with other Christians?
4. Was it proper for Paul to criticize Peter publicly? What does Scripture teach about dealing with erring brethren? with erring leaders?
5. How does one decide whether to make an issue of a doctrinal point, or to accept the fact of different viewpoints so as to maintain peace in the church?
6. What limitations are inherent in the Christian's obligation to be submissive and to follow spiritual leaders? Is any man infallible?
7. If Peter was wrong at Antioch, how can we be sure he was right when he wrote his epistles?
8. How does Paul show that the believer's crucifixion with Christ does not remove personal responsibility for righteous living?

True
Doctrine
Explained
(Galatians 3:1– 4:31)

Chapter 5

The Lesson of Christian Experience

(Galatians 3:1-14)

Because Christian experience begins with the supernatural act of regeneration, it is often helpful in times of spiritual stress to recall one's earliest moments as a newborn child of God. That was the time when, for many at least, the contrast between existence apart from Christ and the new relationship with God through the regenerating work of the Holy Spirit was most sharply distinguished. Remembering one's spiritual beginnings can focus attention on what is essential, and guard the believer against being so swayed by the latest religious fad that he is led astray almost before he realizes it. This was the approach used by Paul in this portion of his letter.

II. TRUE DOCTRINE EXPLAINED (3:1—4:31)

A. The Galatians' Previous Christian Experience (3:1-14)

Paul had been the spiritual father of the churches of Galatia. He knew how they had come into existence, and what transformation had been wrought in the lives of the believers. A reminder of those previous experiences should have been specially effective coming from him, for the readers knew that the writer of this letter had played a vital role in much that had taken place.

1. *They had received the Spirit by faith.* (3:1-5)

VERSE 1. Addressing the readers as "O foolish Galatians," Paul revealed his thinking that their listening to the Judaizers was senseless and irrational. He had already demonstrated how illogical it was to compromise with the principle of grace. His previous statement had shown the implications of the false teaching they were confronting, namely, that Christ had actually died in vain if it were possible to be made acceptable to God by performing the regulations of the law (2:21). In this context one senses more of surprise and sadness than of harsh accusation. To Paul the readers were like children who had failed to use their powers of perception and had been captivated by some persuasive salesmen.

The question "Who bewitched you?" employs a common superstition as a figure to depict the irrationality of the Galatians' fascination for this erroneous doctrine. They were acting as if they had been mesmerized. Paul did not mean it literally, however, for he did not believe in witchcraft, nor the evil eye, nor did he treat his readers as though they were really under some sort of hypnotic spell. He held them responsible for what they were doing, and did not resort to any exorcist methods to relieve them of their ailment. On the contrary, by appealing to their minds, he asked them to remember, to think seriously, and to draw logical conclusions from the facts they knew.

Their folly was all the more inexcusable because Christ had been so clearly and openly proclaimed before them. He had been presented as the crucified Savior whose sacrificial death had satisfied God's righteousness in a way that no system of human works ever could. Paul's previous preaching in the cities of South Galatia had left no doubt among his hearers. He had preached the truth about Jesus Christ, as publicly as the government notices which placarded the buildings of their streets.[1]

VERSE 2. One question would serve to bring the problem into focus. Paul asked, "Did you receive the Spirit as a consequence of performing works of law or by hearing God's word with faith?" He is speaking here of the Spirit Himself,[2] not the various gifts which the Spirit provides for believers. Hence the reference

---

[1]The verb *prographō* is used in the sense of "to write above" (i.e., previously in the same writing), "to write previously," or "to make a public proclamation." The first does not fit the context of Gal. 3:1; the second is ruled out by the accompanying phrase "before whose eyes." The last suits the context admirably; Christ had been clearly presented to them like a posted proclamation. See G. Schrenk, "Graphō, Prographō, *TDNT*, 1, 770-72.

[2]The Greek text employs the article for the phrase *to pneuma*, emphasizing the Spirit's person, rather than the anarthrous form which often connotes the Spirit's demonstrations.

is to the initial reception of the Holy Spirit at regeneration. Further indication that this was Paul's thought is found in the later phrase, "having begun by the Spirit" (3:3). Historically we may refer to the circumstances at Pentecost (Acts 2) and at the house of Cornelius in Caesarea (Acts 10) in order to understand his thought. The answer to Paul's question was obvious. The Spirit who regenerates comes in response to the hearing of the Word of God which is accompanied by faith. Cornelius provides a clear example. He and his household received the Spirit at the moment they believed the gospel, apart from any human effort or demonstration (Acts 10:43-44; 11:15, 17).

VERSE 3. What had occurred with Cornelius had also been true of the believers in Galatia. They too had been born again by the action of the Holy Spirit entering their lives at the moment they had trusted Christ. Paul repeats his word "foolish" (cf. 3:1) to show how senseless it would be to repudiate in principle the very thing which had brought about their new life in Christ. They had begun their Christian life by the reception of the Holy Spirit, an experience which had come by faith, not by keeping the law of Moses. Did they actually think they could be "bringing to completion in the flesh"[3] the process of sanctification which the Spirit had begun? The false teachers in Galatia were insisting that sanctification must be carried on by human efforts, specifically by placing converts under the regulations of the Mosaic Law. "Flesh" is here a reference to man unaided by the Spirit of God. It refers to what is earthly and human; and inasmuch as man is a fallen, sinful being, "flesh" is opposed to the operation of the Spirit. How foolish to suppose that a system which never could bring regeneration to sinners could still somehow bring about their ultimate transformation into the likeness of Christ.

VERSE 4. As the Galatian believers are urged to remember their previous Christian life up to the time when the disturbing pressures began, they should recall also the sufferings they had undergone for their faith. The Book of Acts records some of the sufferings of Paul and Barnabas when they had evangelized that

---

[3]The KJV rendering "made perfect" should be understood either in the passive sense of "made complete," or preferably as a middle "bringing (yourselves) to completion" (epiteleisthe).

area (Acts 13:50; 14:5-6, 19). The sufferings of the Galatian converts are not mentioned, although Paul did warn them to expect
much tribulation (Acts 14:22). Whatever suffering they had experienced, doubtless much had come from Jewish persecutors,
just as in the case of the apostles. If these converts had not fully
trusted Christ for a complete salvation, then they were mixing
grace and law and were not really trusting Christ alone to save
them. Or if they should now revert to a system of law-keeping, in
order to satisfy God's righteousness, they would be repudiating
their former position which claimed that they looked to Christ
alone. Either way the sufferings they had experienced would
have been for nothing. Paul, however, hastens to add, "if indeed
it was in vain" (NASB). The implication is that he doubts that
the readers had really adopted the Judaizers' view as yet. He has
hope that their Christian experience was genuine because their
hope was firmly and completely on Christ.

VERSE 5. Not only had these Galatian readers received the
Spirit and sacrificed their physical well-being in the cause of
Christ, but they had also witnessed other supernatural activity
among them. "He then who provides you with the Spirit" is a
reference to God who supplies believers with the Spirit (Gal. 4:6;
I Thess. 4:7-8). "Provides" is a translation of a Greek word[4]
which originally meant "to stand the expense of bringing out a
chorus" at some festival. The patron bore such expenses as
costuming and training, and usually wanted to appear as lavish
as possible. Hence the term connoted a liberal supply.

They had also witnessed the performance of miracles among
them. The term "miracles"[5] does not necessarily mean more
than "works of power," and can denote spiritually energized
deeds which need not be miraculous. However, "miracles" is a
legitimate rendering in this context. It could refer to otherwise
unknown miracles performed by Galatian Christians. Inasmuch,
however, as miracles seem to be particularly the signs of an
apostle (II Cor. 12:12), it is more likely that the reference is to the
miraculous deeds done by Paul and Barnabas on their recent
visit to Galatia (Acts 14:8-10; 15:12). Such displays had not been
made by the Judaizers who insisted on the works of the law as a

---

[4]Greek: *epichorēgeō*. The word "chorus" is an English derivative.
[5]Greek: *dunameis*.

requirement for Christian living, but by the missionaries who had proclaimed a message which elicited faith from the hearers.

2. They had become sons of Abraham by faith. (3:6-9)

VERSE 6. The experience of the Galatian believers in receiving divine approval because of their exercise of faith had been paralleled by Abraham centuries earlier. A reference to Abraham was appropriate at this point because it was to Abraham that God had revealed Himself and granted the covenant which was later confirmed by the sign of circumcision. One suspects that the name of Abraham figured prominently in the teaching of the Judaizers, who must also have pointed out that it was Abraham's "seed" who were the heirs of the promise (3:16).

Paul quoted Genesis 15:6 which said of Abraham, "He believed God and it was reckoned to him as righteousness." It was Abraham's faith in God's promise which brought the divine pronouncement of righteousness. This was before any meritorious deeds by Abraham. It was long before he offered Isaac. It was more than four hundred years before the Mosaic Law was given (3:17). Nor should it be supposed that his faith was somehow a meritorious "work," for God has done *all* the work. It was God who came to Abraham and offered him the promise. Abraham merely accepted the gift which God offered. He had not earned it nor worked for it in any sense. On the basis of his faith, God treated Abraham as meeting the standards which are required for acceptance with God.

VERSE 7. How may others enjoy the righteousness which God reckoned to Abraham? The Old Testament offered the promise to the heirs of Abraham. But how does one become related to Abraham? Jewish people commonly thought that physical descent was sufficient qualification, but Jesus said that "children" of Abraham are those that exhibit the same kind of trusting obedience to God that Abraham did (John 8:39). Paul says that the true sons[6] of Abraham are those who share his faith. Those

---

[6]It should be remembered that "son of" was a common Semitic expression to denote special characteristics, such as "sons of Belial," or "son of encouragement" (Acts 4:36). R. A. Cole suggests that the meaning here could be "real Abrahams," although he regards the traditional translation as more appropriate because of the context emphasis on descent. R. A. Cole, *The Epistle of Paul to the Galatians* (Grand Rapids, 1965), p. 93.

who are "of faith"—that is, whose relationship to God is derived out of faith—are the ones who enjoy the spiritual kinship with Abraham which brings eternal blessing.

VERSE 8. Thus Gentiles as well as Jews may obtain righteousness because it is received by faith. This was no innovation originated by Paul. It was announced long ago to Abraham, hundreds of years before Moses ever wrote it down in Scripture. The quotation is drawn from Genesis 12:3 and 18:18.

"Preached the gospel beforehand to Abraham" (NASB) is a reference to the announcement made by the divine Author of Scripture. Because "the gospel" has a specialized connotation for Christians, referring to the proclamation of the good news of salvation through the death and resurrection of Jesus Christ, it would be less confusing to translate the Greek text[7] as follows. "The Scripture . . . announced as good news beforehand to Abraham. . . ." The contents of the good news to Abraham of righteousness received by faith, and the gospel of Christ which is preached today are not unrelated, however. The latter is simply a more detailed proclamation which states the means whereby God has made possible this offer of righteousness available by faith to all who will trust the merits of His Son.

The good news of righteousness by faith was not limited to Abraham, for the announcement to him explained that "in thee shall all nations be blessed." In Abraham's day the distinction between Jew and Gentile was not known (even the name "Jew" is derived from "Judah," a great-grandson of Abraham), but the promise to him included blessing for all nations. In the circumstances of God's dealing with Abraham, the enjoyment of a righteous standing with God was certainly a large part of the "blessing" under discussion. "In thee" means "in connection with Abraham," that is, they will be declared righteous by God just as Abraham was—by faith, apart from circumcision or any other rite (Rom. 4:9-12). This would come about because the Messiah, the Seed of Abraham, would provide Himself as the object of men's faith (3:16).

---

[7]The text does not employ the noun *to euangelion*, which would denote a particular message, but the verb *proeuēngelisato*. This fact lends itself to the interpretation given above where the stress is not so much on the content per se as on the action of making a happy announcement.

VERSE 9. The conclusion is drawn, therefore, that Gentiles obtain righteousness as a consequence of trusting God for it, not by observing Jewish practices. They receive by faith the blessing of a perfect standing with God, just as Abraham did. It is those who are "of faith"—not just those of Jewish blood or those who keep Jewish laws—who are the true sons of Abraham. Judaizers, who insisted on imposing Mosaic observances on Gentile believers, had failed to grasp the real heart of the promise to Abraham. It was "the believing Abraham"[8] who received the blessing, and whose spiritual sons all true believers are.

3. *They had been redeemed by Christ from the curse of the law.*(3:10-14)

VERSE 10. The readers' Christian experience should also have taught them that they had been redeemed by Christ from the curse which the law imposed on them. It was the gift of Christ received by faith which had rescued ·them, not any system of law-keeping.

The Judaizing opposition may have taught that Abraham's situation of being declared righteous because he believed God was unique, and that the coming of the Mosaic Law afterward was God's most recent plan to save men. Paul's answer was that the law does not bring God's verdict of righteousness. It brings rather a curse on its violators. This includes everyone under its jurisdiction, for no one ever kept all of its provisions, specially when understood in its essential meaning as explained by Jesus (Matt. 5—7). The apostle cited the passage, "Cursed is everyone that continueth not in all things which are written in the book of the law to do them" (Deut. 27:26). These words were originally spoken as the conclusion to the series of curses that were publicly proclaimed from Mount Ebal on that dramatic occasion when the tribes divided themselves in the valley between Mount Gerizim and Mount Ebal and recited the blessings and cursings which God had promised (see Fig. 7). Thus any who looked to the Mosaic Law for righteousness would find a curse instead, for the law demanded full compliance (see James 2:10-11).

---

[8]The adjective *pistoi* is used here in the active sense "believing" rather than the more passive "faithful" (KJV). This seems clear from 3:16 where it is Abraham's act of believing which is stressed.

VERSE 11. Not only did the law not bring righteousness because no one could keep it, but also because righteousness by this means was never declared by Scripture. On the contrary, the Old Testament taught, "The just shall live by faith" (Hab. 2:4, quoted also in Rom. 1:17 and Heb. 10:38). It never stated, "The just shall live by law." The phrase "by faith" (ek *pisteōs*) can be understood "as a consequence of faith" or "out of faith." Thus there is clear Scriptural warrant for understanding that those whom God calls righteous have their spiritual life as a consequence of faith.

VERSE 12. Furthermore, faith and law are not two sides of the same coin. "The law is not of faith." They are opposing principles. Law is antithetical to faith as a means of justification before God. This is proved by another citation from the Old Testament, "The man that doeth them shall live in them" (Lev. 18:5). The law demands "doing," whereas faith receives as a gift what God has already done. Performance of the requirements of God is a delight to the child of God whose heart has been transformed (Ps. 119:26, 47, 77, 97); but when one relies on his performance of God's demands to earn him salvation, he finds himself falling far short of the perfection which God's holiness

Fig. 7. Mount Gerizim (l.) and Mount Ebal (r.), site of the reciting of the blessings and cursings. *Levant*

requires. Those who are relying on conformity to law to save them are under the curse of God because all men have violated God's law.

VERSE 13. Man's only hope of righteousness is found by another means—in Christ who redeemed the prisoners from the curse of the broken law. "Us" probably refers to Jews who were specifically under the provisions of the Mosaic Law, and hence under the curse for its violation.[9] It was Christ, the Jews' Messiah, who came in fulfillment of the ancient prophecies and particularly of the promise to Abraham; but the merits of His redemptive work have been extended to Gentiles as well (3:14).

The metaphor "redeemed" is not here the purchase of a slave from the market, but of the ransoming of a condemned person from the condemnation of a broken law. Using the Hebrew concept in which the victim on whom the curse rests or the curse offering is identified with the curse itself,[10] Christ is said to have become "a curse in our behalf." The Biblical proof is quoted, "Cursed is everyone that hangeth on a tree" (Deut. 21:23). Criminals who were executed because the law had cursed them were often either hanged or impaled, and their obvious accursed state was such that the law instructed the people to bury the victim the same day lest the land be further defiled. "For us" employs the Greek preposition *huper* in one of its many uses with the sense of substitution (cf. John 11:50; II Cor. 5:20; Philem. 13). The idea of a substitutionary sacrifice is also clear from the context where men who are under a curse are set free from it by Christ who took their place.

VERSE 14. The purpose was that the blessing of justification by faith which Abraham received might be extended to all the nations. This purpose was accomplished by Christ's death at the

---

[9]Although the article is not employed with "law" in 3:2, 5, 10, and 11, thus arguing for understanding *nomos* as the "principle of divine law" rather than as the Mosaic Code specifically, the article does appear in 3:12 and 13. There does not appear to be any great difficulty caused by seeing "us" in 3:13 as Jews, since they are distinguished from Gentiles in 3:14. Inasmuch as the redemption of both Jews and Gentiles is clearly in the author's mind throughout the passage, perhaps he should be conceded a certain generality in his use of the pronouns here.

[10]See Arndt, p. 418. Note also Lev. 4:21-25, where the same word is used for sin and sin-offering.

cross whereby He satisfied the law's curse. Because He was the unique Son of God, the merits of His life laid down as a sacrifice were sufficient for all men, regardless of whether they were Jews or not.

The second part of verse 14 is probably parallel to the first, enlarging on the nature of the blessing of Abraham as including the reception of the promised Spirit who brings regeneration to all who believe.

The passage has shown that all the Galatian Christians, both Jew and Gentile, had received regeneration of the Spirit by faith in Christ's substitutionary work (3:1-2, 14), not by the merits of personal law-keeping. This truth was in harmony with the principle of Abraham's justification, and thus any claims of a Judaizer which regarded faith as insufficient were Scripturally and experimentally baseless.

Questions for Discussion

1. How does a person receive the Holy Spirit?
2. According to Paul, who are the sons of Abraham?
3. What was the good news preached to Abraham?
4. Why are those who seek God's approval by keeping the Law of Moses (or any other system) under a curse?
5. What is the basic difference between law and faith as the means of justification?

Chapter 6

Mosaic Law and the Abrahamic Covenant
(Galatians 3:15-22)

Paul's argument that salvation (that is, righteousness or acceptability with God) is a gift received by faith has been based largely on the dealings of God with Abraham. "Abraham believed God and it was accounted to him for righteousness" (3:6; cf. Gen. 15:6). Such an argument should have carried great weight with both Jews and Gentiles, for it involved God's dealings with a man before there were any distinctions as Jew and Gentile. Thus Gentiles need not feel they were excluded, and even the most ardent Judaizer could not disparage Abraham, for he was revered as the progenitor of the Hebrew people.

Judaizers, however, might insist that the Mosaic Law was God's later revelation to men, and thus was intended to add something new to the simpler basis by which God had dealt with Abraham. This sort of objection was anticipated by Paul, and he dealt with it concisely but convincingly.

B. The Relation of the Law to the Abrahamic Covenant (3:15-22)

1. *The law came later than the covenant and cannot change it.* (3:15-18)

    a. Even human covenants after ratification cannot be changed. (3:15)

VERSE 15. So far from supposing that the Law of Moses made any basic additions to the covenant which provided righteousness by faith, Christian readers must understand that even ordinary human covenants do not operate this way. "I speak after the manner of men" is not an apology nor a disclaimer of divine inspiration for the following words. It is rather Paul's indication that he intends to cite an illustration from human customs. He will remind the Galatians about legal practices with which they are familiar.

Several words in this sentence should be clearly understood. "Covenant" (diathēkē) is the translation of a Greek term which was commonly used of a "last will and testament."[1] Occasionally it was used of a treaty, but only when the terms were largely fixed by one party and imposed on the other. Another term (sunthēkē) was employed in Greek for agreements negotiated by parties on more or less equal terms. The term diathēkē was used in the Septuagint (i.e., the commonest Greek translation of the Hebrew Old Testament) to translate the Hebrew berît (covenant) because the one-sided character of God's covenant was the point to be conveyed. Whether it should be regarded as "testament" or as "covenant" in 3:15 is arguable. Paul's point in this passage does not hinge on this distinction. He is merely calling attention to a properly ratified legal document affecting several parties.

"Confirmed" (kekurōmenēn) means ratified or validated. "Disannulleth" (athetei) means to invalidate a matter, set it aside, or make it void. "Addeth thereto" (epidiatassetai) means to add a codicil, as to a will. Human practice in such matters is that once a legal agreement has been drawn up and properly ratified or validated (such as a will which has been probated), no one is able to make any changes in it unilaterally. In a will this is particularly obvious because one of the principals has died, and thus can no longer be a party to new negotiations. The same is true more generally of other covenants. Once the agreement has been duly recognized as valid, ordinarily neither party can void it nor make changes in it. The application Paul would make of this analogy is clear: The Mosaic Law cannot have affected the basic provisions of the covenant with Abraham. Before Paul did so, however, he demonstrated that the covenant has a direct relevance to the Christian era.

b. The covenant was also for Abraham's seed. (3:16)

VERSE 16. The provisions of the Abrahamic Covenant include a wide variety of promises, such as the enhancement of Abraham's name, a great nation to come from him, blessing for

---

[1]An excellent discussion of diathēkē is found in Johannes Behm, TDNT, 2, 104-34.

all families of the earth, and the land of Palestine as an inheritance for his seed forever (Gen. 12:1-3, 6-7; 13:14-17). Other passages in the Bible indicated that many of these provisions relate exclusively to those who are the physical descendants of Abraham, that is, the Jewish nation. However, the spiritual blessing of Abraham was to be shared by all the nations of the earth in connection with Abraham's "seed," and this did not require that they first become adherents of the Mosaic Law.

The apostle builds his argument on the fact that God's promise to Abraham mentions his "seed" rather than "seeds," and concludes that in the fullest sense Christ must be the Seed before believers can be collected into the "seed of Abraham" (3:29). Paul is often accused of using forced exegesis here, as if he did not know that the Hebrew term (just as the Greek one) was commonly used in the singular as a collective noun. Thus his conclusion has been regarded as unwarranted from the grammatical distinction he was making.

Several factors, however, should be noted. It is obvious that Paul knew that the Hebrew and Greek words for "seed" (zera, sperma) often refer to more than one person, for he himself used the singular noun in a collective sense in 3:29. Nevertheless, both the Hebrew and Greek terms for "seed" can refer to one person. Instances are found of Seth (Gen. 4:25), Ishmael (Gen. 21:13), and Samuel (I Sam. 1:11). Furthermore, Paul surely knew that God had consistently led Abraham to think not in terms of all his offspring, but of a certain one. He was told that his seed would be found in Isaac not Ishmael, even though both were his children (Gen. 17:20, 21). Isaac and Rebekah were likewise told that there would be a distinction made between their two sons Jacob and Esau (Gen. 25:21-23). Therefore, we need not suppose that Paul was interpreting the singular "seed" as Christ exclusively (anymore than Isaac was the exclusive seed of Abraham apart from his own descendants Jacob and the patriarchs), but that Christ was the special Seed to whom others must be united if they are to enjoy the blessing of the seed of Abraham (3:29). Isaac was the special seed of Abraham (Gen. 21:12), but so were others who were related to Isaac (such as Jacob). In like manner Christ was the particular Seed in whom the promise to Abraham would reach its consummation, and

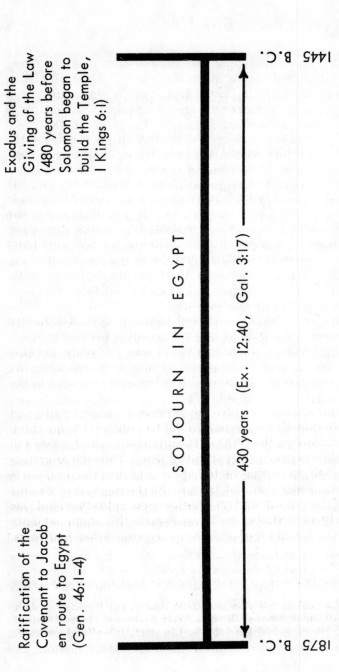

Fig. 8. Time Chart II: Sojourn in Egypt.

Ratification of the Covenant to Jacob en route to Egypt (Gen. 46:1-4)

1875 B.C.

SOJOURN IN EGYPT

430 years (Ex. 12:40, Gal. 3:17)

Exodus and the Giving of the Law (480 years before Solomon began to build the Temple, I Kings 6:1)

1445 B.C.

believers become the spiritual seed of Abraham by being related
to Christ (3:29).

   c. The covenant was ratified 430 years before the law was
      given. (3:17)

VERSE 17. Paul now applied the illustration he made in 3:15.
The Mosaic Law had come into existence long after the covenant
had been given to Abraham. The covenant had been repeated
several times—to Abraham (Gen. 12:1-3, 6-7; 13:14-17; 15:1-21;
17:1-14; 22:15-18), his son Isaac (Gen. 26:2-4, 24), and his grand-
son Jacob (Gen. 28:13-15; 35:9-12; 46:2-4). Yet the law was not
given until more than four centuries after the last confirmation
to the patriarchs. Whatever other purposes the law may have
had, it could not have been intended to alter the basic provisions
of the unconditional promise to Abraham, nor nullify it. God's
very integrity was at stake.

There is a problem involving the number "430 years." The
point of the argument is not affected, but the historical difficulty
of the chronology should be noted. According to Exodus 12:40,
the length of Israel's sojourn in Egypt was 430 years; but this
does not seem to include the previous time in Canaan when the
covenant was given, which would add several centuries to the
total.

Numerous attempts to solve the problem have been made, and
the most frequently suggested should be noted. (1) Some think
Paul was following the LXX[2] of Exodus 12:40, which gives 430
years for the sojourn "in Egypt and Canaan." Thus the prior time
from Abraham to Jacob is included. By this view the problem is
merely transferred from Galatians to the Hebrew text of Exodus
12:40, but it is not solved.[3] (2) Another view holds that Paul was
deliberately understating the figure to make this argument more
forceful. The actual time would have been more than 600 years,

---

[2]The Samaritan Pentateuch is similar but with the locations named in reverse
order.

[3]Among those holding this view are Martin Anstey, *The Romance of Bible
Chronology* (London: Marshall Brothers, 1913), p. 114, and *The New Scofield
Reference Bible*, ed. E. Schuyler English, et al. (New York: Oxford University
Press, 1967), p. 86, n. 2.

but Paul merely cited the well-known figure for the Egyptian portion.[4]

(3) The view most plausible to me regards the 430 as covering the time from the *ratification* of the covenant to Jacob just before he went to Egypt (Gen. 46:1-4) until the giving of the law at Sinai a few months after the exodus (see Fig. 8). This view agrees with the 430 years in the Hebrew text of Exodus 12:40; it understands the 400 years of Genesis 15:13 and Acts 7:6 as the bondage portion of the Egyptian sojourn (the first years under Joseph were prosperous, Exod. 1:7-9), and regards Acts 13:19, 20 as making use of a round number in its computation.[5] If it is objected that the ratification of the covenant to Jacob was not that prominent an event, it should be noted that Galatians refers specifically to the ratification, not the original granting, and Psalm 105:9-10 gives due recognition to the importance of this event.

d. The covenant was a promise. (3:18)

VERSE 18. Inasmuch as later actions cannot invalidate God's covenant, it remains that the promises contained in that covenant are still in effect. The promises had to do with Abraham's "seed" who would inherit the blessings which God had pledged. Now, however, the Judaizers were teaching that in order to inherit these blessings, one must place himself under the authority of the Mosaic Law. This, said Paul, would be a fundamental change. "If the inheritance be of the law, it is no more of promise." When God made the promise to Abraham, He put no requirements on him. The promise was repeated to Isaac and Jacob, and no conditions were imposed. Because the patriarchs believed God's promise, with no strings attached, they had been declared righteous. For anyone to insist that now one

---

[4]This view is held by R. C. H. Lenski, *Interpretation of Galatians* (Columbus, 1946), pp. 162-63.

[5]Among those holding this view are William Hendriksen, *Exposition of Galatians* (Grand Rapids, 1968), pp. 137-39, and Jack R. Riggs, "The Length of Israel's Sojourn in Egypt," *Grace Journal*, 12, 1 (Winter 1971), pp. 18-35. Although drawing a slightly different conclusion, Harold W. Hoehner presents a good discussion in "The Duration of the Egyptian Bondage," *Bibliotheca Sacra*, 126, 504 (October 1969), pp. 306-16.

must place himself under the law in order to inherit the provisions of the promise to Abraham was to place that inheritance on an entirely different basis. It would be "no more of promise." Yet it *was* a promise, for God had "freely given" (*kecharistai*) the covenant to Abraham by a promise. The verb is a word which denotes a free and gracious gift, and the employment of the perfect tense "has freely given" implies that this act produced a condition which is still in force. Consequently, if the covenant with Abraham is valid (and, of course, it is), the law cannot possibly be used in any way as a codicil to it.

2. The law was given to condemn men of sin. (3:19-22)

a. The law gave sin the character of transgression. (3:19)

VERSE 19. The question logically arises: if the law was in no sense an amendment to the covenant of blessing given to Abraham, why was it instituted? Paul's answer was: "It was added because of transgressions." In view of the previous argument Paul has used, it is certain that he did *not* mean the law was added to the covenant as an amendment or codicil. His thought was rather that the law was added to God's revelation to men, and its purpose was next stated.

The translation "because of" renders a Greek word (*charin*) which may denote either cause or purpose. If the former is the intention, Paul's meaning was that the law was given because man's sinfulness was so great. The law was to act as a restraint on him. It is more consistent with Paul's thought elsewhere, however, to regard *charin* as indicating purpose here, so that the meaning is: law came in order that sin might take on the character of actual transgression of clearly indicated standards. Unless there is a revealed law, sin is sinful but it is not transgression (Rom. 4:15). This understanding fits well with Paul's emphasis in this passage, for he was engaged in showing that the law did not make men righteous but served to condemn them (3:22).

"Till the seed should come" shows that the law was also temporary. It was not intended to be God's perpetual regulating force for human conduct. It would serve only until Christ the Seed (3:16) should come. "To whom the promise was made" is a

rather awkward rendering of the Greek text.[6] NASB translates similarly, "to whom the promise had been made." NIV has "to whom the promise referred." Inasmuch as all other New Testament uses of this verb are middle rather than passive, it is certainly possible that this is the sense here; and the meaning is clear: "to whom he [i.e., God] had promised." The promises find their fulfillment focused in Christ, and those who wish to enjoy them must come into relation with Christ. The Mosaic Law had fulfilled its function by making transgression clear.

As Paul referred to the Mosaic Law, he described it as "in the hand of a mediator." The angelic involvement in the giving of the law is not fully explained in Scripture, and yet it was apparently common knowledge among Jews of the first century. Stephen made the same assertion (Acts 7:53) and so does the Epistle to the Hebrews (2:2). In the Old Testament, Deuteronomy 33:2 states: "And he said, The Lord came from Sinai, and rose up from Seir unto them; he shined forth from Mount Paran, and he came with ten thousands of saints [ASV "holy ones"]; from his right hand went a fiery law for them." The Septuagint has for the last clause, "at his right hand were angels with him." Psalm 68:17 says, "The chariots of God are twenty thousand, even thousands of angels: the Lord is among them, as in Sinai, in the holy place."

The mediator of verse 19 is Moses who stood between God and the people and delivered the law to them. This feature will be developed in the next sentence, as Paul shows the subordinate place of the law in relation to the covenant with Abraham.

b. The law was inherently subordinate to the Abrahamic Covenant. (3:20)

VERSE 20. Building on the concept of "mediator," Paul notes that "a mediator is not of one."[7] This is generally true, although

---

[6]Greek: *hoi epēngeltai*.

[7]The Greek text uses the article in the generic sense, "the mediator." The sense is clearly that all mediators by definition imply at least two parties.

Fig. 9. Mosque at modern Konya, site of ancient Iconium, the second city of South Galatia visited by Paul and Barnabas on the First Missionary Journey. *Levant*

Paul has Moses particularly in view. A mediator never acts for himself, but stands in the middle between two or more parties. Thus there is a certain remoteness between the principals when a mediator is used. It was this feature which Paul noted as showing the Mosaic Law to be an inherently subordinate kind in comparison to the covenant with Abraham.

"But God is one." The statement coming as it does at this point in the discussion has stimulated a wide variety of interpretations.[8] The simplest explanation, however, relates it to the contrast between the law and the covenant. The law utilized a mediator between two parties, and this was viewed by Paul as involving a remoteness and hence a certain weakness. But the covenant made with Abraham emanated from God alone. It was unconditional, and its fulfillment was not weakened by having several contracting parties. Since God is one and is immutable, the provisions of His covenant are certain.

Is the force of this argument weakened by the fact that the New Testament also speaks of Christ as a mediator? In fact, every other occurrence of the Greek word *mesitēs* (mediator) in the New Testament refers to Christ (I Tim. 2:5; Heb. 8:6; 9:15; 12:24). The answer must be that Paul understood Christ to be no mere human mediator like Moses. He knew that Christ was God, and thus the distinction he was drawing in verse 20 was legitimate, for "God was in Christ reconciling the world unto himself" (II Cor. 5:19).

c. The law had a purpose different from the covenant. (3:21, 22)

VERSE 21. Inasmuch as the law has been shown to be in direct contrast to faith (3:12), and served to make sinfulness more obvious as transgression of God's specific commands (3:19), the question arises: Is the law then against the promises of God? Are the two so opposed to each other in principle that at least one of them must be evil? Paul regarded any such conclusion as mon-

---

[8]Lightfoot mentions the report of up to 300 interpretations of this passage, *Epistle to the Galatians* (Grand Rapids, reprinted.), p. 146; Ridderbos refers to 430 interpretations, *The Epistle of Paul to the Churches of Galatia* (Grand Rapids, 1956), p. 139.

strous: "May it never be!" (NASB). Both had come from God but they operated in different spheres.

Paul demonstrated this by proposing a hypothetical situation[9] and then showing its falsity from Scripture. Let us suppose for the moment, he says, that God had given a law to mankind which was able to impart spiritual life. If that were so, then assuredly the state of acceptability with God (i.e., righteousness) would be derived out of law. There would have been no need for the gospel which promised eternal life through faith in Christ. People could place themselves under that law (and it was the Mosaic Law specifically at issue) and forget about the promise of righteousness by faith. All they would need to do would be to keep perfectly the requirements of that law as God intended it.

VERSE 22. But what is the actual situation? Paul goes to Scripture itself to show that no one can be made spiritually alive by keeping the Law of Moses (nor any other law).[10] "The Scripture hath concluded all under sin." The verb *sugkleiō* means to close up together, surround, or lock up. It was used of the catch of fish which had been trapped in the disciples' nets (Luke 5:6). Paul used it again in the next verse to describe Jews as held in custody by the law until the Christian faith came (3:23). In the present instance Scripture (i.e., the law) is depicted as locking up in prison all men[11] under the condemnation of sin. The law does not make anybody alive. Rather it puts them all under sentence of death. If one specific Scripture[12] is referred to, it is probably Deuteronomy 27:26 (quoted in 3:10) or Psalm 143:2 (quoted in 2:16), but there are numerous other passages which convey the same thought (e.g., Ps. 130:3; Jer. 17:9).

---

[9]Grammatically a contrary-to-fact condition.

[10]Passages which purport to offer life to men on the basis of keeping the law refer to temporal life and God's blessing on earthly existence (Deut. 8:1). Jesus' statement to the lawyer (Luke 10:25-28) was intended to show the man his inability by causing him to measure himself against the standard of the law. "This do and you will be living" is a legitimate rendering of Luke 10:28, with the sense being that if he actually could perform perfectly all the law, he would show that he already possessed spiritual life. It does not imply that law-keeping would provide life.

[11]The neuter plural *ta panta* means here all men, together with their deeds, thoughts, words, and character.

[12]Commonly the singular articular use *hē graphē* refers to a specific passage rather than Scripture as a whole. However, this rule is not without exceptions (John 2:22; 20:9; James 4:5).

The purpose of the law was to indicate clearly to those under it their state of condemnation before God. Only when this is recognized are men ready to accept the promise which God offers them in Christ. This promise is embodied in the gospel, which holds out to mankind the hope of righteousness based not on law-keeping but on the merits of Christ. The only way to receive the benefits of an unconditional promise is by faith. If one works for it, it is no longer a free gift. But God gives the promise embodying righteousness and eternal life to those who believe Him by exercising faith in the substitutionary work of Christ.

It is evident, therefore, that the function of the law was in no sense in competition with nor antagonistic to the covenant which promised righteousness by faith. Instead, it was God's instrument to show unmistakably man's need for the promise. Righteousness comes only by God's gift, and sinners receive it by faith.

Questions for Discussion

1. Did God ever count men as possessing righteousness on the basis of law-keeping?
2. Why was the Mosaic Law given?
3. What are Paul's reasons for insisting that the covenant with Abraham was not replaced by the Mosaic Law?
4. In what senses is the word "seed" used?
5. How do we know that God's promise to Abraham is still in effect?

Chapter 7

Mosaic Law and the Christian Faith

(Galatians 3:23 — 4:7)

Christians from the beginning have confronted this issue. What is the relation of the believer in Christ to the Law of Moses with its regulations for men? Is the Christian obligated to observe the law except for certain ceremonial elements which are either dropped or "Christianized"? The problem of the Christian believer's relation to the Mosaic Law came up early and frequently in the apostolic church (Acts 11:1-18; 15:1-32; 21:20 ff.). Even though councils were held, epistles were written, and the apostles preached clearly to the church what the truth was on the matter, many Christians even today are confused over this issue. The following passage in Galatians is of continuing relevance, therefore, as Christians seek to direct their lives in accordance with the whole counsel of God in Scripture.

C. The Relation of the Law to Christian Faith (3:23—4:7)

1. *Before the Christian faith came, Israelites were under the law.* (3:23-24)

VERSE 23. In the Greek text "faith" has the definite article: "the faith." Hence it is not a reference to faith in general, for this existed in Old Testament times. "Abraham believed God" (3:6), and every other saved person in the Old Testament was also saved by faith, not by works (3:11). The expression "the faith" should, therefore, be understood in the particular sense of the faith just mentioned in the previous verse: "the faith of Jesus Christ" (3:22). A good translation would be: "Before this faith came." The reference is to the coming of Christ when men had their first historical opportunity to put their faith in Jesus Christ, the crucified and risen Redeemer.

Before the inauguration of the Christian era, "we were kept

Fig. 10. Greek schoolboy and teacher. Terra cotta statuette from third century B.C. *The Metropolitan Museum of Art, Avery Fund, 1923.*

under the law." The reference is obviously to the Jews, of whom the writer was one, who were continually under guard, so to speak. The figure of imprisonment is continued by the expression "shut up" (*sungkleismenoi*), which utilizes the same word that appeared in 3:22 to describe sin as shutting or locking up all men under condemnation. Here it is the law rather than sin which is depicted as the jailer, but these are not totally different, for the law contained the standards which had been transgressed and thus was the proof that sin had been committed.

This guarding of Israelites by the law was temporary, for its termination is indicated by the phrase "unto the faith which should afterwards be revealed." It was in force until the fulfillment of the promise in Christ, until the Christian faith would be unveiled. This, of course, has now come to pass.

VERSE 24. The law guarded and restrained its subjects as a jailer until Christ came. It also acted on those under its jurisdiction as a guardian of minor children. The Greek paidagōgos was not a schoolmaster, but was a slave who had charge of children from the age of seven to about eighteen.[1] He trained the child in general deportment, took him to school each day, saw that he dressed properly, and was in almost total charge of the management of the boy. Sometimes the paidagōgos was a trusted slave who was a true friend as well, but more often he was a slave too old or disabled for any other work. Generally speaking, the connotation of paidagōgos in the ancient world was unsatisfactory. When Paul chose this term for his illustration, he was emphasizing the temporary character of the law and its inferiority. The law was Israel's guardian and trainer until Christ. When the Christian era arrived, justification by faith was made clear, and the inability of the law to provide justification was demonstrated (see Acts 13:39 for another Pauline statement to this effect).

2. *After the Christian faith came, believers received a new position.* (3:25-29)

a. Believers are released from the guardianship of the law. (3:25)

VERSE 25. The coming of Christ ushered in a new era. The inauguration of the Christian faith was like a coming of age for those under the Mosaic Law. They were as children who had now come to maturity and were no longer subject to the continual directives of the childhood guardian. A change had occurred whereby inward transformation and maturing had taken place, and the outward compulsion of the Mosaic Law was superseded by another method in God's dealings with men.

---

[1]William Barclay, *A New Testament Wordbook* (New York, n.d.), pp. 87-90.

b. Believers are constituted as full sons of God. (3:26)

VERSE 26. In contrast to the time before Christ when believers were likened to minors under a guardian, believers are now full-grown sons. Paul has changed from the first person "we" referring to Jewish people under the law (3:23-25) to "ye all," because what he now has to say refers to both Jewish and Gentile Christians at Galatia and elsewhere. All Christian believers, to follow Paul's analogy, are fully acknowledged sons[2] of God, not minor children. This has come about because of the proclamation of the Christian faith which brings its adherents into a vital relationship with Christ Jesus.[3]

c. Believers are identified with Christ. (3:27-28)

VERSE 27. Those who have been "baptized into Christ have put on Christ." Although many interpreters are convinced that the rite of water baptism is in view here, this can hardly be the direct meaning of the words for not everyone who has received water baptism has actually "put on Christ." Even Paul seems to be making a subtle reference to this, for his words "as many of you as have been baptized into Christ" may be intended to distinguish these from others who may only have been baptized in water.

"Baptized into Christ" refers to that act of the Holy Spirit whereby the believer is placed spiritually into the body of Christ and made a sharer of Christ's life (I Cor. 12:13). It denotes all persons who are truly born again. By this supernatural act, they have "put on Christ." This is not a reference, even in illustration, to the donning of white baptismal robes by the candidates for baptism, for such a development was most certainly later than Paul. Most likely it is the characteristic Pauline thought that regeneration by the Spirit clothes the believer with Christ in a vital union (Rom. 13:14; Col. 3:4). If there was any contemporary

---

[2]The Greek text has huioi theou, "sons of God," and this should be reflected in translation in order to preserve the contrast Paul is making between minor children and mature sons.

[3]"In Christ Jesus" (en Christōi Iēsou) should probably not be restricted to "faith" (for which eis would have been expected rather than en) but should be regarded as modifying the whole concept of this sonship. It is because believers are "in Christ Jesus" that they are sons.

custom involved, it was most likely the change in dress which marked the transition from boyhood to manhood. A Roman lad wore the *toga praetexta*, a toga with an elaborately embroidered purple hem. When he reached manhood, he put off this sign of childhood and assumed the pure white toga.[4]

VERSE 28. By being baptized into Christ's body, believers have become a part of a spiritual unity in which human distinctions are irrelevant. Among the members of the body of Christ, the earthly distinctions of race ("neither Jew nor Greek"), social class ("neither bond nor free"), and sex ("neither male nor female") have no significance as to the validity or quality of one's relationship with God. Such divisions are due to earthly realities, and do have validity, of course, in temporal matters. As long as the church is on earth, these distinctions must be recognized and taken into account. The New Testament provides considerable regulation for the church on earth regarding the varying responsibilities of husbands and wives, their relative positions in the functioning of the local assembly, and the duties of slaves and masters toward each other. But so far as the essential character of the body of Christ is concerned, "ye are all one in Christ Jesus." In the believer's spiritual standing, there is unity and an equality. All believers—regardless of race, class, or sex—are equally a part of one spiritual entity. They are all "in Christ Jesus"—in a vital union with Him whereby they share His life, His perfect righteousness, and the prospect of participating in the promises He will receive as the Messianic Heir.

d. Believers are the seed of Abraham. (3:29)

VERSE 29. Because believers belong to Christ in this most intimate way (note the phrases used: "baptized into Christ," "have put on Christ," "in Christ Jesus"), they are constituted as Abraham's seed. Paul has already shown that Christ is Abraham's unique Seed (3:16); and inasmuch as believers are united with Him, they share His position. They did not become Abraham's seed by physical descent, for most of the Galatian Christians were Gentiles. Nor had they become Abraham's seed by keeping the Mosaic Law. No, they had become "heirs accord-

---

[4]W. S. Davis, *A Day in Old Rome* (New York, 1972), p. 83.

ing to the promise." The promise to Abraham of justification by faith and its attendant blessings is shared by those who are in Christ the Seed. The significant fact is that all these benefits are made possible not by the Mosaic Law, for the law could not make men sons of God, Abraham's seed, nor heirs. They are due solely to God's promise which is received by faith.

3. *Childhood versus full sonship illustrates the contrast.* (4:1-7)

a. Before Christ came, Jews were like minor children under guardians. (4:1-3)

VERSE 1. Paul's illustration clarifies the problem which may be raised: if Old Testament saints (not just Jews generally) who were also heirs of the promise had the Mosaic Law, why should not Christian believers also be subject to it? Paul depicts a child who is the heir of his father's estate. As long as the child is a minor, his personal life is little different from a slave in the same household. He is dependent on others for direction and has no control over the estate. These things are also true of his father's slaves. "Though[5] he be lord of all," his childhood prevents him from exercising the lordship that he will someday assume.

VERSE 2. During this period of childhood, the heir is under the supervision of "tutors and governors." The first term (*epitropous*) probably denotes the guardians of the lad himself, and the second (*oikonomous*) refers to managers of his property. These overseers may have actually been slaves, but at the time described they assumed positions which made them temporarily superior to the young heir. All of this was "until the time appointed of the father," the date established for the son to enter into the rights and privileges of his inheritance as an adult son. The illustration is most readily understood if it is assumed that the father had died and had left instructions in his will for the care of his son and the management of his estate. This most easily accounts for the mention of managers of the boy's prop-

---

[5]The circumstantial participle *ōn* (being) is concessive.

erty, as well as the reference to the appointed day.[6] It is not really essential, however, to know whether the father was dead or not, inasmuch as the point of the illustration is not the relation of the child to the father, but of the child to his guardians. (The comparison of the dead father with the living God need not be pressed, for the father is really a minor detail of the illustration. The point lies elsewhere.)

VERSE 3. The illustration is now applied. "We" refers to Paul, the Jewish author of the epistle, and other Jews during the time before Christ. "When we were children" likens the Old Testament economy under the Mosaic Law to the childhood aspect of the illustration. Just as the minor heir was under guardians and managers, so the Jewish people were "in bondage," that is, completely controlled as slaves "under the elements of the world." The word "elements" (stoicheia) occurs seven times in the New Testament.[7] It conveyed such ideas as the elementary principles of learning, the basic physical elements of which the world is composed, and even the heavenly bodies.[8] The expression "elements of the world" occurs three times, all by Paul (4:3; Col. 2:8, 20); and the interpreter is largely limited to the immediate contexts of these passages to arrive at the sense. In the present passage the "elements of the world" are parallel to the tutors and governors of the child during the Old Testament period. Thus the Mosaic Law seems to be involved in some way. The same idea is conveyed in 4:9-10, where the Galatians' contemplated return to the Mosaic ceremonies is termed a return to "weak and beggarly elements." In Colossians 2:8 the "elements of the world" appear to be descriptive of some kind of human philosophy, and Colossians 2:20 speaks of these "elements" as

---

[6] Inasmuch as Roman law specified the age at which a minor orphan was released from his tutor, the date does not seem to be left to the father's decision as in Paul's illustration. However, our knowledge of this law is of a period somewhat later than Paul's day. One could imagine a case of a father away on a journey who anticipated delay in returning and left explicit instructions regarding his young son. E. D. Burton discusses the case of Antiochus Epiphanes who on his departure for a military campaign in Persia, left his son Antiochus Eupator in the care of Lysias as steward and guardian of his son until a specified time (I Macc. 3:32-33; 6:17). Epistle to the Galatians (Edinburgh, 1921), pp. 214-15.

[7] Galatians 4:3, 9; Colossians 2:8, 20; Hebrews 5:12; II Peter 3:10, 12.

[8] Arndt, p. 776.

religious teachings from which the readers had supposedly been separated through their union with Christ. In the verses immediately preceding, some of those teachings clearly involved Jewish ceremonies (Col. 2:16). Therefore, the expression as used by Paul seems to denote the regulations of the Mosaic Law, and particularly the ceremonial and other earthly features which the law obligated men to do.

b. Since Christ came, believers are like full-grown sons. (4:4-7)

VERSE 4. The coming of Christ is described as occurring "when the fulness of the time came" (NASB). Paul does not elaborate what made the time "full." Many have noted the numerous providential factors that were present at that time. The Greek language was understood throughout the Mediterranean world, making evangelism more convenient. The Roman Empire united the world under one government and built a remarkable system of roads which greatly facilitated travel. The presence of synagogues throughout the empire provided a base for Christian preaching and meant that the Old Testament Scripture was known and available almost everywhere. Paul, however, probably had in mind primarily the fact that from God's standpoint the time was ready.

"God sent forth his Son." Christ's preexistence is strongly suggested here, for the Son is not only sent by God but "out from" God (*exapesteilen*). Thus the Son is described as being sent out from His preexistent state into the world. This understanding is confirmed by Paul's teaching elsewhere (I Cor. 8:6; Phil. 2:6-8; Col. 1:15-16).

Two descriptions of the divine Son are given. The first, "made of a woman" (KJV; "born of a woman," NASB), accords well with the New Testament teaching of the virgin birth of Jesus, and has often been used as an indication that Paul believed and taught this doctrine. The phrase,[9] however, is very similar to

---

[9] Greek: *genomenon ek gunaikos* (Gal. 4:4). The fact that Paul uses *ginomai* and the other passages cited use forms of *gennaō* proves nothing, for both terms can mean "born" (cf. John 8:58), and both are used elsewhere of Christ (Matt. 1:16; John 18:37).

Christ's own description of John the Baptist as among the greatest of those "born of women"[10] (Matt. 11:11), and to Job's description of man as "born of a woman"[11] (Job 14:1). Neither of those statements is ever interpreted as depicting a virgin birth. Consequently, it is more likely that the emphasis here is on Christ's genuine humanity; for the passage is showing Christ's condescension and likeness to us, not His dissimilarity. He was "born of woman," just as all men are.[12]

Likewise, in the second description, He was "made under the law" (KJV; "born under the Law," NASB), just as all Israelites were. Both of these descriptions depict the incarnation of Christ, showing to what extent the Son of God went in order to identify Himself with mankind. Jesus was born as a Jew subject to the Mosaic Law, and He kept its requirements perfectly. This made possible the purpose of His coming which is next stated.

VERSE 5. "That he might redeem those who were under the law" is parallel to the thought of 3:13, where Christ is said to have redeemed Israel from the curse of the law. Now if Jesus by His death redeemed Israelites from the law's authority and penalty, it should be obvious that Gentiles (such as the Galatians) who had never been under the Mosaic Law would certainly not be obligated to that law now. This redemption from the law was for the purpose of granting the beneficiaries "adoption as sons" (NASB). Those under the law were like minor heirs, potentially wealthy but practically little different from slaves (4:1-3). Christ's act of redemption provided all that was necessary to release men from the law's claim on them, and enabled believers to be treated as sons of full age, no longer under a guardian. "Adoption as sons" is etymologically "placing as sons," and refers to the conferring of the rights of sonship. Here it describes the believer's installation as a full son after the period of childhood (represented by the law) was past.

VERSE 6. An accompaniment of this position as sons of God is the inner testimony provided by the Spirit who assures the

---

[10]Greek: en gennētois gunaikōn (Matt. 11:11).

[11]Greek: gennētos gunaikos (Job 14:1, LXX).

[12]This explanation does not imply that Paul was unaware of the doctrine of the virgin birth, for he was acquainted with the apostles and later had Luke as his close companion for many years. The virgin birth accounts appear at length in the Gospels of Matthew and Luke.

believer of his sonship. Because the fact is true that "ye are sons," God has sent into the hearts of all believers the "Spirit of his Son." This is another name for the Holy Spirit, who is also called sometimes the Spirit of Christ (Rom. 8:9) or the Spirit of Jesus (Acts 16:7). The indwelling Spirit prompts the filial cry "Abba, Father" (compare Rom. 8:15). "Abba" is the Aramaic word for "father," and Paul has given both the Aramaic and the Greek terms. Mark did the same thing as he recorded the prayer of Jesus in Gethsemane (Mark 14:36). The expression may have been a frequent one in the prayers of early Christians, for *ho patēr* (Father) does not appear to be a mere editorial note in our passage to translate an unfamiliar word *Abba*, but represents part of an actual expression used by Christians generally. It is expressive of the intimate feeling of sonship experienced by all Christians as they recognize the reality of their new position.

The shift in the persons of the pronouns in this passage from "we" (4:3, 5) to "you" (4:6) should be noted. The most obvious explanation of the "we" in this section refers it to Jewish people under the Mosaic Law prior to Christ's coming. "You" refers to the Christian believers at Galatia, composed mostly of Gentiles but including some Jews. By Paul's explanation, it is shown that every Christian believer has the position of a full-grown son of God, whether he is Jew or Gentile. In answering the question of how the Mosaic Law fits into the picture, he has shown that it was a temporary measure given to the Jewish people for a period that he likened to childhood under a guardianship. Now, however, all believers since Christ are "sons" in the full sense.

VERSE 7. The explanation is summarized and Paul's conclusion is applied individually as he changes from the plural "you" of verse 6 to the singular in verse 7: "Thou art no more a servant but a son." This answers the question why the law is not binding on Christians as it had been on Old Testament saints. The period of the law's guardianship ended with Christ's coming. Full sonship is the present believer's experience. And by virtue of having the status of a son, the believer is thereby an "heir through God."[13] The maturity achieved in Christ is due to God

---

[13]This translation is based on the preferred reading as found in P 46 ABC. So NASB.

who commissioned His Son (4:4) and the Spirit (4:6) to bring it about. The believer, then, is an heir to the promises to Abraham and his seed (3:19), not on the basis of subjecting himself to the Mosaic Law, but by receiving through faith the gospel of Christ.

Questions for Discussion

1. What was the purpose of the Mosaic Law? Did it have more than one purpose?
2. In what sense are there no racial, social, or other distinctions "in Christ"?
3. What are the practical implications of "putting on Christ"?
4. Can you suggest why Christ came at the particular time He did?
5. Why does Paul say that Christians are not subject to the Mosaic Law?
6. What advantages does adoption as sons of God provide?

Chapter 8

The Folly of Returning to the Law

(Galatians 4:8-20)

Religious ritual has a fascination for many. Pageantry, festivals, ceremonies, and symbolism quickly capture the imagination. Religious feelings can be stirred by certain music, or awakened by the sight of a stained glass window or a spire. In contrast, the emphasis on truth and faith and worship in the spirit can appear drab and unexciting. Nevertheless, ceremonies and spiritual worship are not necessarily antagonistic. Spiritual truth can be taught in symbol and ceremony. The Old Testament did much of this, and Jesus gave His church certain ceremonies to perpetuate.

The fact remains, however, that it is possible to observe the ritual and miss the truth. People have often satisfied themselves that performance of ceremonies is all that God requires, and have missed the very heart of what true worship of God is all about. The reason is that usually a participation in ritual is much less demanding than submission of one's life to God and a daily walk in conformity with His Word. There can be an aesthetic satisfaction in religious pageantry, and this may be sufficient to ease the individual's desire for some religious activity without much personal inconvenience.

The Galatians were being tempted along these very lines. The Judaizers had apparently presented the attractive features of the Mosaic Law with special emphasis on the festivals and ceremonies (4:10). The less attractive observances, particularly circumcision, had not yet been adopted by the readers (5:2), but the other celebrations were proving most alluring. Paul in this section pleads with his readers to see the folly of this course of action.

D. The Folly of Returning to the Law (4:8-20)

1. *Returning to the law was inconsistent with their Christian experience.* (4:8-11)

   a. The Galatians had previously worshiped things which were not true deities. (4:8)

VERSE 8. Paul has primarily in view the Gentile converts in Galatia, who were doubtless far more numerous than the Jewish Christians there. They had been enslaved to the worship of the idols of false religions. Even the Jewish Christians, however, were for the most part unsaved before they heard the gospel,[1] and thus the religious area of their lives had been misdirected. They had not known God in any saving way either, and thus their worship had been mere ritual.

Paul and Barnabas had firsthand experience of the idolatrous practices at the Galatian city of Lystra, where they almost became the unwitting guests of honor at a pagan sacrifice (Acts 14:11-18). This fanatical devotion to false religion is denoted as a kind of slavery[2] ("you were slaves to," NASB).

   b. Now they had come to know the true God. (4:9a)

VERSE 9a. By trusting Jesus Christ, they had come to know God (John 14:6). The days of their spiritual ignorance were supposedly past. Coming to know God brings regeneration, spiritual enlightenment, and a new direction to life. The believer has been made a new creature (II Cor. 5:17). Knowing God is the very essence of eternal life (John 17:3), and this had come about in Galatia when Christ had been preached by Paul and Barnabas.

Lest it be supposed that the Galatians' knowing God was in any way the product of their own efforts, Paul clarifies the point by adding, "or rather are known of God." God's foreknowledge

---

[1]At this time of transition it was still theoretically possible for an Old Testament believer to be found who had not yet had his belief in God heightened to the full dimensions of Christian faith.

[2]Greek: *edouleusate*. "All of the words in this group serve either to describe the status of a slave or an attitude corresponding to that of a slave." Karl H. Rengstorf, "Doulos, *et al.*," *TDNT*; 2, 261.

of the believer is the significant factor in the believer's knowing God. Being known by God, according to Scripture, involves much more than acquaintance or awareness. When God said of Israel, "You only have I known of all the families of the earth" (Amos 3:2), He meant that Israel had been the recipient of His favorable regard which had acted on their behalf, in contrast to other nations which He had not "known" in this special way. The Galatian believers likewise had been known by God and made the objects of His saving grace.

    c. To subject themselves again to pre-Christian obser-
       vances was inconsistent. (4:9b-11)

      1) Such observances were rudimentary and weak. (4:9b)

VERSE 9b. Paul seems almost mystified as he asks the question, "How is it that you turn back again?" A return to ceremonies, rituals, and physical celebrations was a step backward. How could the readers even contemplate such a step in view of their present Christian position?

The word "elements" (*stoicheia*) was used earlier in 4:3 ("elements of the world") to describe the various ceremonies of the Mosaic Law which men were obligated to perform during Old Testament times. In that context, these "elements" were characterized as belonging to Israel's period of religious childhood; but now believers are no longer under that sort of guardianship for they have the position of full-grown sons. In 4:9 these ceremonies are further described as "weak" because they are powerless to provide the redemption men need, and "beggarly" because they are poverty-stricken when it comes to supplying the spiritual riches which God has promised.

Paul cannot understand why the Galatians should want to "slave all over again"[3] for these things, after they had once been set free. Inasmuch as these "elements" are clearly a reference to Jewish ceremonies, why does Paul say to the Galatians (largely former pagans who had never been under Jewish law) that adoption of these ceremonies would be to revert to such things "all over again" (NASB)? The best explanation is that even for Gen-

---

[3]Greek: *palin anōthen douleuein.* The verb is the same as in 4:8.

tile Christians to adopt Mosaic practices would be to restore the old pattern of ceremonies which paganism also had. A Jew who performed his ritual without faith in God was actually doing the same thing the pagan did—practicing religious acts of a ceremonial kind which had no efficacy per se.

2) They involved Jewish celebrations. (4:10)

VERSE 10. The similarity to another of Paul's lists in Colossians 2:16 makes it obvious that Jewish rites are in view. "Ye observe" (paratēreisthe) uses the present tense of the verb, showing that the movement toward adopting Jewish ceremonies was already going on and had proceeded this far. However, absence of any mention of circumcision indicates that the defection had not yet reached this point (cf. 5:1-3).

"Days" refers to the observance of Jewish holy days such as the weekly sabbaths and special feast days. "Months" were the celebrations of the new moons which began each month of the Jewish lunar calendar (Num. 10:10; 28:11; I Sam. 20:5, 18, 24; II Kings 4:23; Isa. 1:13, 14; Ezek. 46:1, 3; Hos. 2:11; Amos 8:5). "Seasons" (NASB) were perhaps the festivals such as the week-long Tabernacles and Unleavened Bread, as well as other times of fasting and prayer. "Years" refers either to sabbatical or Jubilee years, or perhaps to the annual celebration of the New Year (Rosh Hashana). For Gentile Christians to begin observing these Jewish celebrations was to embark on a procedure with far-reaching implications, more so than if Jewish Christians simply continued to practice their ancestral customs (as for example, Acts 21:20). It would mean that they thought there was still some religious validity about them that obligated Gentiles to perform them.

3) To adopt such practices would nullify Paul's labor among them. (4:11)

VERSE 11. The seriousness of the situation must not be doubted. "I fear for you, that perhaps I have labored over you in vain" (NASB). If this attraction to Jewish ceremonies should persist, it could lead to an adoption of Judaism in toto, including circumcision and all the rest. Such a turn of events would mean that Paul's labors to establish churches in Galatia based on the gospel of salvation by faith in Christ would have been for nothing, for the churches would be abandoning the principle of grace and would be turning to a system of righteousness by works which has never saved anyone. At this point in the letter, Paul voices his greatest discouragement over the situation in Galatia. Yet he is not without hope, for the word "perhaps"[4] (NASB) qualifies the otherwise bleak outlook. The final outcome sketched above may not occur. The Galatians may yet see the error of the false teaching they confronted and cast off the practices they had begun.

2. *Returning to the law was contrary to their former attitude toward Paul.* (4:12-20)

   a. The Galatians had made no reprisals against Paul in the past. (4:12)

VERSE 12. In the succeeding verses Paul appeals to the Galatians to keep the same attitude toward him they had displayed when he first came among them. He calls them "brethren," perhaps to remind them that his harsh words just preceding did not mean that he had rejected them as Christian brothers. "Become as I, because I also [became] as you" is a literal rendering of the Greek text. English, however, must supply a verb for the second clause. "Became" is the most obvious verb to be inferred inasmuch as it was the same verb used in the first clause. Paul meant that when he visited Galatia he had laid aside his Jewish practices and lived as a Gentile. He became as the Gentile Galatians in their freedom from Mosaic practices. Since then, the Judaizers had influenced some of the Galatian converts to adopt portions of the Jewish religious system. Paul begs them to abandon these things as he had done and live in the freedom made possible in Christ as he was doing. He reminds them, "You did not wrong me."[5] When Paul had been present in the cities of Galatia, they had seen his manner of life. This had not resulted in

---

[4]The particle *pōs* (perhaps) has been reflected in the NASB rendering but not in KJV. Its presence serves to qualify somewhat the fear that is expressed.

[5]The aorist indicative *ēdikēsate* (wronged) points to the past occasion of Paul's visit among them.

Fig. 11. The Mound of Lystra (Zoldran), third of the Galatian cities visited by Paul. *Burdick*

any reprisals against him by the Christians. They apparently found no fault with even a Jewish Christian (i. e., Paul) living in freedom from Jewish ceremonies.

b. They had received him as an angel of God. (4:13-15)

VERSE 13. Quite the contrary, instead of finding fault with Paul when he was with them, they had welcomed him even when he was physically not at his best. He reminded the readers that it was "because of a bodily illness"[6] that he had evangelized them originally. The Book of Acts does not speak of this illness. From the context in Galatians, it is clear that the ailment caused him to be in Galatia to preach, and that the ailment might have led the people to despise him but they did not. One can only speculate, and William Ramsay's conjecture is more plausible than most. He suggests that Paul contracted malaria in the lowlands around Perga, and was compelled to go to the higher elevation in Galatia ahead of schedule in order to recover.[7]

"At the first" (*to proteron*) is urged by some to mean "the

---

[6]Greek: *di'astheneian*. The use of *dia* with the accusative regularly denotes cause. Efforts to treat the phrase as stating a mere accompanying circumstance are not as likely to be correct as those which see the phrase as naming the cause of Paul's first preaching in Galatia.

[7]William M. Ramsay, *St. Paul the Traveller and Roman Citizen* (Grand Rapids, reprinted.), pp. 92-97.

former of two visits."[8] If this is so, then Paul must have visited Galatia twice prior to the writing of this epistle. This does not settle the question of the date of writing, however, for Paul actually visited the Galatian cities twice on the first journey. Hence the epistle could have been written any time after that. However, the more general sense of "formerly" is a common use of this expression and fits well here. The reference is clearly to Paul's initial visit to Galatia. (See Introduction, "Date," for discussion of this problem.

VERSE 14. The Galatians had not allowed Paul's unpleasant ailment to tempt them to reject him. The best textual evidence supports the translation "your temptation" or "the temptation of you" rather than "my temptation." The reference is to Paul's physical affliction which might have tempted them to disregard him and his message. A sick man is rarely impressive. As Lenski has pointed out, a man who claims miraculous power to heal others but remains sick himself raises doubts about any message he might preach.[9] Nevertheless the Galatians had not "despised" him, that is, "treated him as nothing" (exouthenēsate) nor "rejected" or "loathed" him (exeptusate, literally, "spit out").

Rather, they had received him as an angel or messenger from God. Paul's reception in Galatia is described in Acts 13:43-49. Those who became Christians responded to Paul as warmly as they would have to Christ Himself (cf. Matt. 10:40). In one of the cities of Galatia (Acts 14:8-18), some of the misguided residents thought Barnabas and Paul were Zeus and Hermes, and consequently were about to offer sacrifices to them! Whether Paul had that incident in mind here is difficult to say, but at least the point is clear that he was not despised when he had come among them.

VERSE 15. Paul can only wonder what happened to their former joy at the blessing of God. A literal translation of his words is, "Where then is your blessedness?" The noun "blessedness" (makarismos) belongs to a word group in the

---

[8]So J. B. Lightfoot, *The Epistle of St. Paul to the Galatians* (Grand Rapids, reprinted.), p. 175; R. C. H. Lenski, *Interpretation of St. Paul's Epistles to the Galatians, et al.* (Columbus, 1946), p. 219.
[9]Lenski, *Interpretation of Galatians*, p. 220.

New Testament which usually refers to the sense of religious joy which the saved person has.[10] The teachings of the Judaizers were in contrast to Paul's gospel of grace, and yet it was Paul's teaching which had brought blessedness to the Galatians. Why would they turn away, first from the truth which had brought the blessing of salvation and real joy, and then from the faithful apostle who had brought the message to them?

The Galatians' genuine appreciation of Paul initially was no passing fancy. "Ye would have plucked out your own eyes and have given them to me." The eyes are here a metaphor of a priceless possession (as in Deut. 32:10; Ps. 17:8; Zech. 2:8.)[11] The distressing thing was that this joyful attitude—which once would have made almost any sacrifice for Paul—was gone, or nearly so.

c. Paul's blunt speaking was not hostility. (4:16)

VERSE 16. "Am I therefore become your enemy?"[12] It is true that Paul had been speaking bluntly to them about the seriousness of the problem and of his genuine fears for their spiritual welfare. This had been true in the earlier portions of this letter. It may also have occurred when he saw them last and warned about the "much tribulation" through which believers enter the kingdom of God (Acts 14:22). Perhaps word had reached him that the Galatians were calling him their enemy, either because they knew he would oppose their present course, or else because he had not placed them under Mosaic Law as the Judaizers had insisted was necessary.

---

[10]F. Hauck, "Makarios, Makarizō, Makarismos," *TDNT*, 4, 367.

[11]Although this reference to the eyes is used by some to identify Paul's ailment as ophthalmia (e.g., F. Rendall in "Epistle to the Galatians," *EGT*, 3, 178-79), it is precarious to base such a view on this proverbial expression. At this point in the discussion Paul was no longer discussing his ailment but the Galatians' affection for him.

[12]Burton and Rendall argue that the statement is not a question but a declaration, because *hōste* is not used elsewhere in the NT to introduce interrogation (E. D. Burton, *Epistle to the Galatians*, [Edinburgh, 1921], pp. 244-45; F. Rendall, "Galatians," *EGT*, 3, 179). If so, the statement must still reflect the Galatians' point of view, not Paul's, for he was not basically hostile to them. The clause is treated as a question, however, by KJV, ASV, NASB, Nestle, and the United Bible Societies' text.

"Because I tell you the truth" was poor grounds for imagining hostility on Paul's part. Many times the truth may be painful, but it may be the most valuable thing a friend can impart. Merely telling people something favorable because it is what they want to hear may be temporarily pleasant but ultimately disastrous. It does no good to insist that all is well when the house is on fire. Paul's blunt assessment of the Galatian problem was not prompted by hostility, but by the most earnest desire to establish his readers more firmly in the faith.

d. Their real enemies were the Judaizers. (4:17-18)

VERSE 17. The verb "zealously affect" (KJV; Greek: zēlousin) is neutral and denotes a deep concern for someone, without implying whether the purpose is good or bad. In its archaic meaning the word "affect" meant to strive after, but it no longer conveys this sense in modern English. A better rendering would be "zealously court" or "eagerly seek" (NASB). The Judaizers were zealously courting the favor of the Galatian Christians, but their motives were not honorable. The intention was "to shut you out in order that you may seek them" (NASB). By teaching that believers who did not keep the Mosaic Law were on a lower plane and not worthy of full fellowship, they hoped to cause the Galatian converts to be ostracized from Paul. Paul would be blamed for causing their trouble. They might even feel that unless they adopted Judaistic legalism they would be excluded from Christ. The Judaizers were hoping that this wedge they were driving between the Galatians and Paul would ultimately cause the confused believers to turn to the Judaizers and adopt their legalistic message.

VERSE 18. "It is good always to be eagerly sought in a commendable manner" (NASB). Paul does not want it thought that he is moved by mere jealousy that some of his followers had begun looking to other teachers. Therefore he clarifies the principle involved. He himself had zealously sought to gain converts in Galatia, and in turn he had been courted by these eager disciples. His message, however was *good* because it was the gospel authorized by Christ. Thus it was not the zealous courting which was wrong but the perverted ends to which it had been put. Unfortunately, now that Paul was gone from Galatia,

the eager interest of some of those converts had turned elsewhere.

e. Paul longs for Christ to be formed in them. (4:19-20)

VERSE 19. The manuscripts vary between "my children"
(*tekna mou*) and "my little children" (*teknia mou*), although
either would be an expression of endearment here.[13] Using a
metaphor of childbirth, he said he felt as if he was suffering birth
pangs for them again. This time, however, it was not in order to
bring them to Christ. That had occurred when he evangelized
them previously, and thus he could call them his "children."
Now he was suffering an equal spiritual anguish "until Christ be
formed in you." The word "formed" (*morphōthēi*) denotes the
development and display of an outward appearance which
properly represents the inner nature. Inasmuch as they were
Christian believers, Christ already was "in" them (Col. 1:27).
What was needed was a display of the characteristics which
their new life in Christ should have been producing. Maturity in
the faith, rather than vacillation or toying with legalism, is the
form which Christians should display. This is another way of
stating the truth already set forth in 2:20: "Christ liveth in me,
and the life which I now live in the flesh, I live by the faith of the
Son of God."

VERSE 20. The verb *allassō* can mean either "change" or "exchange," and thus Paul has been understood to be saying either
that he wished to "change" his tone to a gentler one, or else to
"exchange" his pen for the living voice by his actual presence.
Both ideas seem to be implied by the context. He clearly states
that he wished to be present with them, rather than depend on
written communication. But it is also reasonable to infer that
Paul hoped by his presence to deal with the situation more
directly and effectively so that he could achieve the positive
results which would gladden his heart and soften his words.

---

[13]Grammatically, *tekna* (or *teknia*) can be vocative, indicating direct address and
the beginning of a new sentence: "My children, ..." This creates an awkward-
ness because of *de* ("but") in v. 20 which normally indicates a new sentence.
NASB handles the grammar as a broken construction and inserts a dash before
v. 20. Another possibility is to regard *tekna* as accusative in apposition with
humas ("you") at the end of v. 18: ". . . with you, my children, regarding whom
I suffer birth pangs. . . ." In the latter arrangement, v. 20 begins a new sentence.

Another visit was not possible at this time, although Paul sincerely wished it[14] to relieve his perplexity over the Galatians. According to the view of the date and circumstances discussed in the Introduction, this epistle was written from Syrian Antioch just prior to the Jerusalem Council. Paul and Barnabas were faced with serious problems at this very time in the Antioch church (Acts 15:1-2). However, Paul did revisit the Galatians some months later (Acts 15:36—16:5).

Thus the folly of returning to the law has been sketched. Through the gospel the Galatians had been brought from enslavement to nonexistent gods and endless ceremonies to the knowledge of the true God. This glorious experience had been the cause of much blessedness and had caused them to esteem Paul as an angel of God, even as Christ Himself. Now to abandon all this in favor of some teachers with selfish designs, to regard Paul as their enemy, and to return once more to legalistic practices, was foolishness indeed. Today's readers often confront the same basic issues, and can find in Paul's discussion the true assessment of the problem.

Questions for Discussion

1. How far had the Galatians gone in their adopting of legalism?
2. Were there any similarities between Jewish ceremonies and paganism?
3. Why do people often resent being told the truth about their errors?
4. Can you name instances where Christians today perform religious ceremonies as a duty without any Biblical authority?
5. What is meant by having Christ "formed" in the believer?
6. What characteristics of the man Paul are seen in this passage?

---

[14]The imperfect tense form *ēthelon* is voluntative, expressing a modified wish, qualified by implied conditions: "I could wish."

Chapter 9

Abraham's Two Sons

(Galatians 4:21-31)

"A picture is worth a thousand words." The same is true of a word picture. A story which illustrates a truth is often just what is needed to clarify the point that has been logically explained. An image sketched for the mind will usually remain long after a detailed argument has been forgotten. So it was that Paul climaxed his treatment of the problem with the Judaizers in Galatia by relating a well-known incident from the Old Testament and using it to illustrate the truth he was emphasizing.

The apostle has sometimes been accused of resorting to a questionable method of rabbinical exegesis in this passage. The rabbis were fond of allegorizing Scripture, using this procedure to extract all sorts of teachings from the ritual or historical passages. Often the interpretations so devised were fanciful and utterly foreign to the meaning of the text under study. Such interpretation was not actually derived from the text but rather imposed on it. When men seek novel interpretations and find "types" everywhere, they are in great danger of imposing their own notions on the plain sense of Scripture. Paul, however, did nothing of the sort. What he did was to sketch the essence of the historical event in order to provide a picture of the sonship of Isaac in contrast to the slave status of Ishmael as illustrative of the problem in Galatia. The illustration served as a reminder that those who insisted on tracing their sonship from Abraham must reckon with the fact that Abraham had two sons, but only one of them inherited the promises. Those who demanded a system of law-keeping for salvation in contrast to those who recognized their status as freemen in Christ were exhibiting the same difference as that between Ishmael and Isaac.

E. The Allegory of Abraham's Two Sons (4:21-31)

1. *The historical facts* (4:21-23)

Fig. 12. Desert region near Beersheba, setting of the Hagar and Ishmael episode. *Levant*

a. The illustration in the law (4:21)

VERSE 21. The word "law" appears twice in this verse. The first instance is without the article and thus is qualitative in its emphasis. It speaks of law as a principle. Hence, "ye that desire to be under law" refers to those who have an interest in imposing some sort of legalistic scheme on themselves. It also indicates that it was not yet an accomplished fact, but still in the "wishing" stage. In Galatia, however, the particular system of law which the converts were contemplating was the Mosaic Law; so Paul asks, "Do ye not hear the law?" Here the article appears with "law," making it clear that the Mosaic instrument is in view. Inasmuch as the incident about to be cited occurred in Genesis 16, long before the legislation was given at Sinai (Exod. 20), it is clear that "the law" refers to the entire Pentateuch or Torah, the divine instruction given to Israel particularly in the writings of Moses. Those who were so eager to place themselves under the authority of law needed to understand the implications of such action, as revealed by the particular law which the Judaizers were promoting.

b. Abraham's sons from two women (4:22)

VERSE 22. Although Abraham had other sons at a later time by Keturah (Gen. 25:1-2), only Ishmael and Isaac, the sons by Hagar and Sarah, are in view in Paul's illustration. "The one by a bondmaid" was Ishmael, born to Hagar the Egyptian slave girl. The story is told in detail in Genesis 16. She was Sarah's slave who had been given by her childless mistress to Abraham in hopes that at least an offspring could be obtained by proxy, a custom paralleled elsewhere in Genesis (Rachel, 30:3; Leah, 30:9) and in neighboring cultures.[1] "The other by a freewoman" was Isaac, born to Sarah, the wife of Abraham, who was of course a free woman (Gen. 21:1-3). The contrast between the two mothers is the slavery of the one and the free status of the other

---

[1]According to the Babylonian Code of Hammurabi (par. 146), a childless wife could give her husband a slave girl for the producing of a son, and could subsequently demote her to slave status again but not sell her if she tried to grasp equality with her mistress. Similarly, the Nuzi texts cite the law requiring a childless wife to provide a slave girl as a concubine for her husband. E. A. Speiser, *Genesis* in The Anchor Bible series (Garden City, 1964), pp. 120-21.

(it is not the fact that one of the women was not a wife, but that she was a slave). Because of the different status of the mothers, the sons had a different status even though Abraham had fathered both of them. Ishmael was born in slavery, but Isaac was born free.

c. The son from the slave woman (4:23a)

VERSE 23a. The child of Hagar was born "according to flesh."[2] Ishmael had been conceived and born in a perfectly natural and ordinary way. There was nothing supernatural about his physical birth. It was the result of a physical union between Abraham and Hagar, accomplished in conformity with the social customs which existed in that day and which would not have caused Abraham's contemporaries to view the circumstances as particularly unusual (see footnote 1).

It is possible to regard "flesh" here as not merely referring to Ishmael's birth as the product of human physical action but as a reference to sinful scheming. Often "flesh" is used in Paul's meetings with an evil connotation, referring to man's fallen nature which is in opposition to the Spirit of God. It is true that Abraham and Sarah grew impatient and took matters into their own hands in attempting to bring about the fulfilment of God's promise to provide an heir. Thus the birth of Ishmael was not only an ordinary physical procreation, but was the result of mere human planning which failed to wait for God's time and direction. However, Paul does not make any point of the sinfulness involved, but rather of the slave status of Hagar, and hence the simpler meaning of "according to flesh" as referring to ordinary human physical effort illustrates Paul's point very well and is preferable here.

d. The son from the free woman (4:23b)

VERSE 23b. The child Isaac born to Sarah involved direct supernatural intervention. He was born "by promise." There was a direct promise made to Abraham and Sarah about the birth of this son (Gen. 18:9-10). Furthermore, although Abraham

---

[2]Greek: *kata sarka*.

fathered Isaac, there was a divine restoration of procreative powers in the bodies of both Abraham (Heb. 11:12) and Sarah (Gen. 18:11; 21:1-2). Isaac's birth was also a physical one as was Ishmael's but it had the added element of God's promise and God's empowering to bring it about. It is thus a strikingly apt illustration of those whose birth originates from above in contrast to those whose birth is only physical and natural.

2. The interpretation of the symbols (4:24-27)

a. These women represent two covenants. (4:24a)

VERSE 24a. When Paul says, "which things are an allegory," he did not deny the historicity of the story. As a Jew he (as well as his Judaizing opponents) believed firmly that the narratives regarding Abraham, Sarah, and Hagar were factual events. Here he means that they can be understood as having also another meaning.[3] He was not supporting the idea that there are hidden and unrelated "spiritual" meanings to be found beneath the plain sense of every passage of Scripture (as Philo did with the Old Testament and Origen did with the New). Rather, he is using the historical incident as an illustration by showing the very principle involved in those actions by Abraham, Hagar, and Sarah.

It is not proper to regard this episode as a Biblical "type," which was a divinely intended resemblance or foreshadowing in the Old Testament of a truth fulfilled in the New Testament era. As an illustration of a principle, however, it is an excellent example. What Paul did here was as much inspired of God as the historical account in Genesis. Christians should beware, on the other hand, of modern "spiritualizing" of Scripture, regardless of how well meant it may be, if it gives a meaning to the Biblical passage which is different from the plain sense of the text.

"These women are two covenants" (NASB). "Are" is used in the sense of "represents," a common use of the verb "to be."[4] The women Hagar and Sarah are explained as representing two

---

[3]The Greek verb is *allēgoreō*, to speak with another meaning, to speak allegorically.

[4]For instance, when Jesus said of the bread at the Last Supper, "This is my body," He meant that it represented His body (Matt. 26:26).

ways that God has employed to deal with mankind, the ways which Paul has been discussing in the previous portion of this epistle.

b. Hagar represents the covenant of bondage. (4:24b)

VERSE 24b. The Mosaic Law given to the Jewish people at Mount Sinai is represented in this allegory by the slave mother Hagar. Just as the offspring of a slave woman was also a slave, so those who have obligated themselves to serve the law are in bondage to the demands of that law and its penalty. The law covenant imposed on all of its adherents a servitude which could not be broken by the individual himself (3:10).

c. Hagar's spiritual descendants represent apostate Judaism. (4:25)

VERSE 25. "This Hagar is Mount Sinai in Arabia."[5] "This Hagar" (to de Hagar) uses the neuter article with the feminine name, and thus the meaning must be "this name Hagar," and is further indication that Paul was not thinking of Hagar so much as a person here but as a symbol in the allegory he was constructing. In the preceding verse Hagar had been connected with Sinai. Here the additional note is given that Sinai is in Arabia. It was thus not a part of the land which had been promised to Abraham and his seed.

In this allegory, Sinai "corresponds to the present Jerusalem" (NASB). The verb means literally "to line up with" or "to belong to a series with."[6] Thus as the comparison is developed, Hagar is in the same series with Sinai; and the series also includes the earthly Jerusalem, which Paul regards as the chief example of the legalism under discussion. It might be charted as follows:

HAGAR = SINAI   = EARTHLY   = THOSE
         COVENANT   JERUSALEM   ENSLAVED
                                         UNDER LAW

---

[5]Numerous textual variations occur in this clause, but the translation of KJV and NASB is supported by the preferred reading in the United Bible Societies' text.
[6]Greek: sustoichei.

Jerusalem, the holy city of Judaism and much revered by the Judaizers, is said to be actually "in bondage with her children." Far more serious than her political servitude to Rome was her spiritual enslavement to the system of the law which was powerless to save from the clutches of sin or the prospect of penalty. By her subjection to the law with its condemnation, Palestinian Judaism was an apt symbol of all who look to mere ceremonies and traditions for their spiritual help.

d. Sarah represents the covenant of freedom. (4:26)

VERSE 26. The allegorical series which proceeds from Sarah culminates in the identity of "Jerusalem which is above" as the spiritual mother of those who look for their justification on the basis of faith. This series of symbols proceeds thus:

SARAH =	COVENANT = OF PROMISE	JERUSALEM = ABOVE	THOSE BORN FREE IN CHRIST

The reference is not to some future Jerusalem, as one might have expected from the previous mention of the "Jerusalem which now is" (KJV). Rather, the contrast is between the earthly legalistic system represented by Palestinian Jerusalem, and the spiritual regeneration which comes from above but which is the present possession of all true believers. Abraham by faith looked for this city (Heb. 11:10). There are future aspects to the heavenly Jerusalem (Rev. 21:2), but many of its spiritual blessings are enjoyed by believers today. Already they are spiritually with Christ "in the heavenlies" (Eph. 2:6), and are said to have come to "the heavenly Jerusalem" (Heb. 12:22). This Jerusalem from above belongs to the series which proceeds from Sarah, the free woman. Hence this heavenly Jerusalem and those who belong to it are free from the shackles which enslave those in bondage under the law's condemnation. It represents the source of the believer's spiritual life as resultant from God's promise, in contrast to natural or legalistic means.

e. The prophecy of Isaiah 54:1 (4:27)

VERSE 27. Paul cites Isaiah 54:1 because it graphically described the restoration of Israel to the position of favor with her

Lord. This cry of rejoicing depicted in Isaiah is based on the death and resurrection of the Suffering Servant in the passage immediately preceding (Isa. 53:1-12). Hence the fruitfulness mentioned in Isaiah 54:1 must have reference to the great increase in believers justified by faith in Christ. The language of the prophet employed for its metaphor the barrenness of a woman whose ultimate progeny became more numerous than those of some other woman. There is good likelihood that Isaiah actually had Sarah in mind, for she and Abraham had been mentioned previously in the prophecy as the ancestors of Israel (Isa. 51:2). With this understanding, the meaning of the phrases is clear. Israel, which had suffered much during her apostate days including the captivity, was like Sarah the long-barren wife of Abraham. There would come a time, however, when Sarah "the desolate" would have more children than her rival. Inasmuch as this prophecy immediately follows the prediction of Messiah's death and resurrection (Isa. 53:10-12), Paul understood the fulfilment as involving the inclusion of all who receive salvation by faith, and this included Gentiles also as the spiritual seed of Abraham. This was occurring at the very time Paul wrote.

"She who has the husband[7] refers to Hagar who temporarily had the use of Sarah's husband. Referring to the two series in Paul's allegory, one recalls that the series which began with Sarah culminates in those who are born free in Christ. The other series which began with Hagar concludes with those enslaved under the law. The former would eventually far outstrip in numbers the latter, for Christian believers were being made everywhere, but Judaism was not growing in any comparable way.

3. The application to the readers (4:28-31)

a. Christian believers are children of promise. (4:28)

VERSE 28. "And you, brethren" (NASB) follows the preferred reading (instead of "we").[8] In spite of the fact that most of the

---

[7]Greek: *tēs echousēs ton andra*.

[8]"You" (*humeis*) is supported by P[46] B D, and is adopted by Nestle and the United Bible Societies' text.

first readers of this epistle were Gentiles, they had become Abraham's seed by faith (3:29). Not only so, but they belonged to the spiritual line of Sarah and Isaac, and were "children of promise." As Isaac was born not by mere natural causes but by the promise of God which not only foretold the event but provided the power to make it possible, so Christian believers (whether Jewish or Gentile) are the result of God's grace, not the product of natural effort. Their spiritual birth was God's doing received by faith, not the result of human effort such as performing deeds of the law.

b. Christian believers are persecuted by those of the flesh. (4:29)

VERSE 29. Ishmael was the one "born after the flesh" (4:23), and his persecution of Isaac centuries before had its counterpart in Paul's day. The incident in view was Ishmael's mocking of Isaac at the time of celebration when Isaac was weaned (Gen. 21:9). Ishmael was fourteen years older than Isaac (Gen. 16:16; 21:5), and at the weaning feast he may have been about seventeen. His "mocking" was apparently much more serious than an innocent teasing. William Hendriksen has pointed out that the same Hebrew verb[9] was used to denote the "jesting" with which Lot's prospective sons-in-law responded to the prophecy of Sodom's doom (Gen. 19:14); it names the accusation against Joseph by Potiphar's wife (Gen. 39:14), the hilarity of the Israelites around the golden calf (Exod. 32:6), and the amusement of the Philistines with their prisoner Samson (Judg. 16:25).[10] None of these instances were mere playfulness. Ishmael may well have realized that Isaac's presence dashed any hopes he may have had of being Abraham's heir.

The one "born after the Spirit" denotes Isaac, whose birth was the result of direct supernatural action on Sarah and Abraham. It is possible that pneuma should be translated "spirit" (rather than "Spirit") as a reference to that God-conscious element in Sarah and Abraham which responded in faith to the promise about Isaac. Even so, the Holy Spirit was doubtless God's Agent

[9]Hebrew: ṣāḥaq.

[10]William Hendriksen, Exposition of Galatians (Grand Rapids, 1968), p. 186.

to bring about the birth of Isaac, so that the Holy Spirit would have been involved in either case.

"Even so it is now." Just as Ishmael had engaged in persecuting Isaac, so Jewish legalists were the chief antagonists of the early church in harassing Christians who did not observe the law. Most of the instances of persecution in Acts were initiated by Jews who violently opposed the gospel of grace (Acts 4:1-2; 5:17-18, 40; 6:9-14; 7:54-60; 8:1-3; 9:1-2, 29; 13:45-51; 14:2, 19; 17:5-7, 13; 18:12-17; 20:3; 21:27-30; 23:12-13; 24:1).

    c. Scripture commands the "casting out" of the slave system. (4:30)

VERSE 30. Again Paul appeals to the very language of the narrative from which he has made this allegory. Sarah became incensed at the mistreatment of her son Isaac by the older Ishmael, demanding of Abraham that Hagar and Ishmael be dismissed from the household (Gen. 21:10). There was a deep concern on Sarah's part that Ishmael might somehow take a share of the inheritance which was due to her free-born son Isaac. Scripture records not only the request of Sarah but also the confirmation of her request by God (Gen. 21:12). Hence this demand for expulsion was no mere jealous petulance but it had the authority of God to support it, and Abraham complied with it.

The lurking fear of a diminished inheritance for Isaac comes out clearly in the emphatic negative of the quotation: "The son of the slave woman shall in no way[11] inherit with the son of the free woman." They had two entirely different standings and the procedures for inheritance left the matter in no doubt. Only trouble was in store if the slave and the free son dwelled together. The older Ishmael must have clearly understood that he had no chance as an heir as long as Isaac was alive, and this created a danger for the child Isaac. The only safe course was to remove the slave boy and his mother from all contact with young Isaac.

    d. Christian believers have no slave mother. (4:31)

---

[11]Greek: *ou mē.*

VERSE 31. The point of the entire allegory is summarized here. "Wherefore, brethren" (dio, adelphoi), gathers together what has been stated, draws the conclusion from it, and then encourages the readers to accept it by addressing them with the endearing name "brethren." Christians, he says, are not "children of a slave woman." No article is used with "slave woman," and thus Paul has in mind not just the particular woman Hagar, but any slave woman of any kind. It is the fact of "slavishness" that is emphasized. "But of the free woman." Here the article is used, pointing to the free woman Sarah and the series of allegorical identifications related to her and culminating in "Jerusalem which is above." This is the only true source of spiritual life, and only those who are related to this spiritual mother can be heirs in God's household. Legalists will not inherit the promises for they will ultimately be removed from whatever superficial and earthly attachment to the household of God they may happen to have. No Christian, therefore, should allow the subtle arguments of the legalist to place him under the Old Testament system of law or any other scheme, as if one could win God's verdict of righteousness by performing deeds of law. In Christ believers have been set free and are not slaves but sons.

Questions for Discussion

1. In what ways does Hagar illustrate those who trust in works of law?
2. In what ways does Sarah illustrate those who trust God alone for salvation?
3. What is "Jerusalem which is above"?
4. Can you name any systems of law-keeping which pose a threat to believers today?
5. In what sense are believers "children of promise"?
6. Why are legalists incompatible with those who trust Christ alone?
7. What is the proper method of interpreting Scripture?
8. Is it profitable to search for hidden meanings in Scripture?

Christian Practice Exhorted

(Galatians 5:1:—6:10)

Chapter 10

Stand Firm in Freedom

(Galatians 5:1-12)

Freedom is a noble ideal. Its practice, however, is not as easy as the shackled slave imagines. Many a freed slave has thrilled at the thought of emancipation, only to be overwhelmed at the personal responsibility he assumes when he is actually set free. More than one freedman despaired of coping with life on his own and sought to return to his former status where the master provided all his needs (cf. Exod. 21:2-6). The Israelites in the wilderness frequently stated their preference for returning to Egypt (Exod. 14:12; 16:3), rather than to remain free.

Freedom brings with it personal responsibility. It demands that the free man make his way as a mature person, not dependent on other people to make his decisions for him or direct every activity. The prospect can be frightening to the immature, regardless of how attractive he may suppose the absence of restraints would be. This is no less true in the religious realm. The Galatian believers, so recently set free from sin by their trust in Christ, were now acting as though they were still dependent on some system of rules and ceremonies to make them acceptable to God. Paul, therefore, begins his transition in the epistle from doctrinal explanation to practical exhortation by urging the readers to stand firm in their new freedom.

III. CHRISTIAN PRACTICE EXHORTED (5:1— 6:10)

A. Exhortation to Stand Firm in Freedom (5:1-12)

1. Christ's purpose in redemption (5:1a)

VERSE 1a. This verse is such an excellent transition between the previous passage and the exhortation which follows that not all agree on where the new thought actually begins.[1] A further

---

[1]E. D. Burton treats the verse as an independent paragraph, not a part of either the foregoing or the following matter (*The Epistle to the Galatians*, Edinburgh, reprint ed., 1971, p. 270). R. A. Cole attaches it to the preceding paragraph (*The*

complication is the rather extensive number of textual variants in this short clause.[2] The preferred reading yields the translation: "For this freedom[3] Christ set us free." Paul has just explained that Christians are spiritually in the line of Sarah, the free woman (4:31). The redemption which Christ secured at Calvary had as its purpose this freedom which constitutes us full freeborn sons of Abraham. This freedom delivered its beneficiaries from the servitude to sin which had once bound them, and also from the subjection to the Mosaic Law which had held them in its debt. Christ set free those who trust Him because He paid in full their penalty and made possible the release of men from the power of sin in their lives.

2. The need to resist reenslavement (5:1b-6)

VERSE 1b. In view of the redemption in Christ, Paul exhorted the Galatians, "keep standing firm" (NASB). They must not waver in their trust, nor wonder whether faith alone could save them. Certainly they must not be "subject again to a yoke of bondage." Inasmuch as most of the Galatian Christians were Gentiles for whom adoption of Judaism would not be "again" but a new experience, it is significant that "yoke" has no article. It was not merely "the yoke" of the Mosaic Law which must be avoided but "a yoke"—that is, any legalistic system, whether Mosaic, pagan, or any other. The same thought was expressed in 4:9, where these former pagans who were contemplating adoption of Judaism were described as "again" about to become slaves of ritual and ceremony. The superficial attractions of pageantry and religious tradition must not be allowed to blind their minds to the fact that behind it all lay a life of bondage. They would become slaves to a system of law which would only

---

Epistle of Paul to the Galatians, Grand Rapids, 1965, p. 136). F. Rendall makes the break after 4:30, and sees the next paragraph as including 4:31—5:12 ("The Epistle of Paul to the Galatians," EGT, 3, 183). Herman Ridderbos (The Epistle of Paul to the Churches of Galatia, Grand Rapids, 1956, p. 186) and E. F. Harrison ("The Epistle to the Galatians," Wycliffe Bible Commentary, Chicago, 1962, p. 1294) treat it as the beginning of a new paragraph.

[2]The United Bible Societies' text lists seven different readings in the first clause of 5:1, and twenty additional minor variations within the seven.

[3]The Greek tēi eleutheriai is probably a dative of advantage, and the article denotes previous reference (4:22-31).

condemn them, and never set them free (3:10). How different is the "yoke of Christ," for it brings ease and rest, not bondage (Matt. 11:28-30).

VERSE 2. "I Paul say unto you." This emphasis on the author himself may be a reminder to his readers of his apostolic authority. He was not merely one Christian talking to another, but was an apostle of Christ, chosen directly by Him and given the gospel by supernatural revelation (1:11-12). It is also possible that these words are an indirect refutation of the Judaizers who had used his name falsely to support their views.[4] What follows would make perfectly clear Paul's view of circumcision. J. B. Lightfoot has noted that the emphatic expression "I Paul" occurs in II Corinthians 10:1 when Paul is combating the criticism of his enemies.[5]

"If ye be circumcised" implies that the circumstance has not yet occurred.[6] The passive voice may be an instance of the causative or permissive passive,[7] so that the sense is "if you let yourselves be circumcised." He is not talking about Jewish Christians who had experienced this rite in infancy (as had Paul himself), but about Gentile converts who were contemplating the practice. The present tense of the verb suggests that circumcision was not being viewed here as simply an isolated act (for which the aorist subjunctive would have been more appropriate) but as a practice or way of life. The readers had not yet gone this far. The reference in 4:10 omits circumcision from the Jewish rites already adopted by the Galatians.

Any who adopted circumcision because they thought it was necessary or helpful in establishing a right relationship with God were totally wrong. In such cases, "Christ shall profit you nothing." The reason is that salvation by Christ would be repudiated, for its very heart is its insistence that human efforts to achieve righteousness by performance of the Mosiac Law or any other system are doomed to failure and condemnation. Man's

---

[4]See comments on 1:10.

[5]J. B. Lightfoot, *The Epistle of St. Paul to the Galatians* (Grand Rapids, reprint ed.), p. 203.

[6]Greek, *ean peritemnésthe*. A third class condition, utilizing the subjunctive mood.

[7]A. T. Robertson, *A Grammar of the Greek New Testament in the Light of Historical Research* (Nashville, 1934), p. 816.

only hope is to receive salvation on the merits of Christ and His redemptive work. If human works provide even the smallest part of man's salvation, then salvation is no longer by grace through faith. The two ways are mutually exclusive.

VERSE 3. For emphasis, Paul repeats the assertion of the previous verse and enlarges on it. Not only is everyone who lets himself receive circumcision thereby turning away from the free gift of Christ, but he is also obligating himself to keep the *whole* Mosaic Law. Circumcision was not merely one item of legalistic observance, but was the sign that one had adopted all of Judaism. A Gentile who received religious circumcision became thereby a full proselyte and was obligated to conform to all the law as fully as any Jew. This question would be thoroughly aired at the Jerusalem Council,[8] where the issue was clearly settled that no Gentile believer should have this burden placed on him.[9] At that council, however, it was obvious that those who insisted on circumcision understood that the entire Mosaic Law was involved (Acts 15:5).

VERSE 4. The two systems of law and grace are antithetical. To adopt one is to be severed from the other. "Whoever of you are justified by law" (KJV) must be understood as the conative use of the verb "justify," which depicts attempted action. The sense is, "whoever are trying to be justified by the law." Paul has previously stressed the fact that no one is actually justified by law-keeping (3:11), but the Galatians who were enamored with Judaism mistakenly thought it could be done.

Inasmuch as law and grace are opposing methods of receiving righteousness, those who pursue the law-keeping method have been "severed from Christ" (NASB). The verb "severed" (KJV: "became of no effect") is used in Romans 7:2 of the woman whose husband's death severed her from the law which had bound her to him (see also Rom. 7:6). By no longer trusting Christ alone, the individual has "fallen from grace." Anyone who adopts a scheme of works for salvation has abandoned the way of grace which God provided. Paul is not discussing salva-

---

[8]Those who date the epistle during Paul's third journey will, of course, regard the Jerusalem Council as having already occurred.

[9]For a more complete discussion, see H. A. Kent, Jr., *Jerusalem to Rome* (Winona Lake, Ind. 1972), pp. 120-29.

tion per se but the two proposed *ways* of salvation. Because these ways are opposites, the adoption of one is the repudiation of the other. If deeds of law are trusted for justification, then of necessity Christ is not. By turning to the principle of circumcision for salvation, one turns away from the principle of grace.[10]

VERSE 5. True Christians are those who by the Holy Spirit are awaiting by faith the public declaration of their righteousness. "We" includes Paul and the Galatians. He has not written off any of his readers as yet, but claims them all as fellow believers in Christ. The "if" of 5:2 is still a warning, not a tragic accomplishment.

"Through the Spirit"[11] and "by faith" express the means whereby Christians expect to receive the consummation of salvation. Rather than embarking on a course of legal duties which never promise the final approval of God, Christians have put their faith in the gospel of Christ and have believed the promise of God. They have been born from above by the supernatural work of the Holy Spirit (note the analogy with Isaac's birth, 4:29). This contrast between the law and the Holy Spirit is a frequent one with Paul, and has been clearly demonstrated by William Hendriksen who shows that the law produces death but the Spirit makes alive (Rom. 8:2, 3); the law produces slavery and fear but the Spirit brings hope (Rom. 8:15, 16); the law enslaves but the Spirit brings freedom (Gal. 4:24, 25, 29—5:1).[12]

"The hope of righteousness" is the expectation of the final public acknowledgment by God of the believer's acceptability with Him. Righteousness is already the believer's possession in justification, but its full realization will be experienced at Christ's coming to claim His own. For this the believer waits in faith. No performance of law could ever achieve it.

VERSE 6. For those "in Christ Jesus," that is, true Christians, circumcision or its absence was immaterial to the securing of any spiritual benefit. In a similar discussion in I Corinthians 7,

---

[10]This passage is therefore not discussing an individual's personal relationship to God ("falling from grace"), but his relationship to the principle for receiving salvation.

[11]The Greek is *pneumati*, a dative of agent.

[12]William Hendriksen, *Exposition of Galatians* (Grand Rapids, 1968), p. 197.

Paul puts circumcision in the same category as slavery and marriage (7:18-19, 21, 27). They were outward conditions which may be appointed for some, but they provide no spiritual merit or demerit. Paul demonstrated his commitment to this principle in his own conduct. He refused to allow Judaizers to force circumcision on the Gentile Titus,[13] but he had the rite performed on the half-Jew Timothy for reasons unrelated to the Judaizing controversy (Acts 16:3).[14] He did not lose sight of this important truth during the heat of argument (as men are often accustomed to do) and support the other extreme that uncircumcision is preferable. Neither condition was preferable because both were irrelevant to gaining merit with God.

What really matters is "faith working through love" (NASB). Faith accepts the promise of God which offers salvation on the merits of Christ. This kind of faith, however, is no barren assent to a creed, but a vital trust in God which brings a new birth to the believer and produces in him a fruitful spiritual life. This faith is "working" and is thus in perfect harmony with the Epistle of James which declares that the only kind of faith which saves is the kind which works (James 2:14-26). By a working faith which produces the fruit of love, the spiritual heart of God's law is fulfilled (5:14), far better than the imposition of the Mosaic Code on Christians could accomplish.

3. The nature of the trouble in Galatia (5:7-9)

VERSE 7. By the use of what Lightfoot calls "St. Paul's favorite metaphor of the stadium,"[15] the author characterizes the trouble that confronted the Galatian Christians. Athletic events were a prominent part of the Greco-Roman world (see Fig. 13), and although Jews generally refused participation or even attendance because of the nudity of the athletes, Paul's frequent athletic metaphors reveal an interest, specially in the footrace. Perhaps this is one area where he demonstrated his emancipation from some of the traditions of his ancestors.

---

[13]See comments on 2:3 ff.

[14]The view of the date of Galatians adopted in this commentary regards Timothy's circumcision as occurring when Paul visited Galatia a few months following the writing of this epistle.

[15]Lightfoot, Galatians, p. 205. He cites as other examples Gal. 2:2; I Cor. 9:24-27; Phil. 3:14; II Tim. 4:7.

Fig. 13. Starting blocks at the race course in ancient Corinth. *Kent*

"You were running well" (NASB). The imperfect tense denotes the running as already begun. The reference is to their Christian life up until recently. They had begun their Christian life in proper fashion by trusting Christ and living in harmony with Christian teaching. Something, however, had interfered with their progress during the interval of Paul's absence. The author asked literally, "Who cut in on you so that ye began[16] disobeying the truth?" As a runner who has been bumped and deflected from the course, they were proceeding along lines at variance from the truth of the grace of God. They were by no means out of the race, but they had made a start in disobedience by mixing some of the Mosaic ceremonies with their Christian faith (4:10). Because "who" is a singular pronoun in the Greek text, it is possible that one Judaizing promoter is specifically in view. However, other references to the agitators are plural (1:7; 4:17; 5:12; 6:12-13), and it is best to regard the singular here as simply indefinite or illustrative.

VERSE 8. A wordplay occurs between the words "obey" (*peithesthai*, v. 7) and "persuasion" (*peismonē*). An attempt to reproduce it in English would be: "You began to be unpersuaded to the truth. This persuasion. . . ." The phrase "this persuasion" refers to the Judaizers' efforts to introduce legalism into the Galatian churches. "Him that calleth you" denotes God who had called them to salvation (1:6) and continues to call them to trust Him. It was certainly not God who had been responsible for the Judaizers' message, for theirs was a different gospel from the good news of God's grace in Christ. Nor could it have been simply a further development in God's revelation to men, for it was opposed in principle to salvation by grace through faith, and God does not contradict Himself. The introduction of any kind of mandatory works would mean that salvation was no longer a gift. If it can be worked for, then salvation becomes in some sense wages. Yet Paul has clearly shown that those who hope to find God's approval by their works will find only a curse instead (3:10-11).

VERSE 9. At present the trouble in Galatia was small, but it was

---

[16]The present infinitive is regarded as inchoative, describing the action as beginning (4:10), but not as proceeding yet as far as circumcision.

in danger of spreading like yeast in a batch of dough. "A little leaven leaveneth the whole lump" seems to have been a proverb, and Paul used it also in I Corinthians 5:6. In ancient times, housewives kept a small batch of dough from a previous baking, allowed it to ferment, and then kneaded it with the flour in their next baking to make leavened bread.

"Leaven" was regarded in Old Testament ritual as symbolic of corruption (probably because it implied disintegration and corruption, and hence uncleanness), and was prohibited at Passover, the Feast of Unleavened Bread, and for most of the offerings. The New Testament likewise uses leaven as a symbol of evil,[17] and particularly of evil doctrine. Jesus spoke of the leaven of the Pharisees and Sadducees, and showed that He was referring to their false doctrine (Matt. 16:12). Inasmuch as Paul has explained that the Galatians were being persuaded not to obey the truth (i.e., true doctrine), it is consistent with the other New Testament uses to regard leaven here as referring to the Judaizers' doctrines. Already the Galatians had received "a little leaven," for they had adopted some legalistic practices (4:10). Hence Paul is extremely concerned, not because all the Galatians had abandoned the faith, but because he knew the permeating and corrupting effect of false teaching, and he was aware that already a foothold had been gained.

4. Paul's confidence in the outcome (5:10-12)

VERSE 10. The danger to Galatians was great but Paul's confidence in them was greater because it rested ultimately "in the Lord." He believed that his readers were truly saved, and were themselves "in the Lord." Consequently his trust was not in the outward appearances which were disconcerting at the moment, but in the Lord who is always faithful to His promises and preserves His own. This encouraged Paul to believe that the Galatians would not finally adopt the false teaching of the Judaizers. He was confident that they would recognize the truth of his warning just given in 5:9 that even a little bit of legalism is

---

[17]The only possible exception to this evil connotation is in Jesus' parable of the leaven (Matt. 13:33; Luke 13:21), but many interpret this use also as symbolic of false doctrine existing in the present form of the kingdom.

potentially disastrous. They would "think nothing other" (*ouden allo phronēsete*) than the true doctrine which had originally been preached to them and which Paul had now reemphasized.

As for the promoter(s) of error, however, their prospect was sober indeed. The singular form "he that troubleth you" (*ho de tarasson*) could conceivably point to one particular ringleader whom Paul knew to be the source of the trouble in Galatia. However, the further designation "whoever he may be" is indefinite, and 5:12 uses the plural "those who are troubling you" (NASB). Hence it is better to regard the statement as a general indefinite mention. Whoever the enemy was, whether one or many, God would deal with him. He could not find escape in pleading good intentions or failure to hear the truth. The guilty must bear his guilt.

VERSE 11. The guilt of these false teachers is demonstrated by the obvious falsity of some of their accusations. "If I yet preach circumcision" suggests that Paul was accused of being a promoter of Jewish practices just as he was before his conversion and in spite of what he was now saying. It seems incredible that anyone would seriously entertain such a notion; yet it has already been noted that Paul was accused of altering his message in order to be popular with his audiences (see comments on 1:10). Instances from various times and places in Paul's career reveal how Judaizers could misunderstand the principle involved and hence might use it against him. He had the half-Jew Timothy circumcised, not to win favor with God or place him under the law, but to make him more acceptable among unconverted Jewish people (Acts 16:1-3). Although Paul was accused of teaching Jewish converts to abandon the law and reject circumcision, this was apparently incorrect, and Paul engaged in a Mosaic ritual to prove he had not demanded that Jewish Christians reject their traditions (Acts 21:21-26). Nevertheless the undiscerning might construe such actions as a promotion of the law.

Paul's answer was, "If I am really advocating circumcision, why do I experience all this persecution?" Most of it was from Jewish opponents, but they would not have opposed him if he were on their side. The fact of his persecution by the Jews should surely cancel the charge that he was proclaiming circumcision as required for salvation. If he actually were preaching circumcision, the "offense of the cross" would no longer be irritating the Jewish community. The preaching of the cross was the proclamation that the Messiah had died in a despised way, but that His death was the expiation for sin which enables men to be saved by faith. If circumcision could provide this, the cross was unnecessary. Thus if Paul had been promoting circumcision, the offensiveness of the cross in his Christian preaching would have been nullified to the Jews and Paul would have escaped persecution. Such was clearly not the case.

VERSE 12. These words seem harsh by contemporary standards. Nevertheless the most literal translation is: "Would that those who are troubling you would even mutilate themselves" (NASB). The verb "cut off" (KJV) is the term for castration or similar mutilation in Deuteronomy 23:1 (LXX). Such physical mutilation for religious purposes was commonly known in Galatia, being practiced in the worship of Cybele. Paul's irony meant: If these Judaizers regard the physical act of circumcision as a saving rite, they may as well go all the way and imitate their pagan neighbors, for in principle they were no different. In another epistle Paul referred to this wrong emphasis on physical circumcision as "the mutilation" (Phil. 3:2).

Every Christian needs to understand that his hope of righteousness with God is based on no merits of his own, but on the perfect righteousness of Christ. Any attempt to place men back under a system of laws designed to win righteousness is contrary to the purpose for which Christ died. He set believers free so that they might walk in the freedom which belongs to sons of God. Stand firm, therefore, in this freedom, says Paul, and resist every attempt to reenslave you.

Questions for Discussion

1. Why is legalism a "yoke of bondage"?
2. What did Paul mean by "fallen from grace"?
3. Why is Christ of no value to those who adopt legalism?
4. What is the relation of faith and love?
5. Why was Paul persecuted so violently?

Walk by the Spirit

(Galatians 5:13-26)

Freedom from enslavement is one of man's highest aspirations. Bondage imposes restraints which usually prevent the development of one's full potential. Freedom, therefore, whether it is political, economic, social, or religious, has always excited the heart of man and prompted him to strive for it, no matter how remote the accomplishment might seem.

Absolute freedom, however, is not without its problems. The greatest danger is its potential for abuse. The libertine hungers for freedom so he can use it for selfish indulgence. The legalist is afraid of it for that very reason. The church of Paul's day confronted this issue early in its experience, and Paul's answer is still the clearest explanation of the principle which should underlie all Christian behavior.

What is the Christian view of the believer's conduct? Is there a way to be free from the Mosaic Law and yet not be as sinfully unrestrained as the licentious pagan? Is there a more effective way to develop godly living than by imposing a legal code on the Christian? Paul's answer takes full cognizance of man's problem, but explains that the only way to live properly before God is to walk by the Spirit.

B. Exhortation to Walk by the Spirit (5:13-26)

1. The caution against license (5:13-15)

VERSE 13. It is true that the effective call of God which brings believers to Christ has also brought them freedom (see 5:1). "You were called to[1] freedom" (NASB). This involved freedom from

---

[1]The preposition *epi* with the dative here indicates purpose, goal, or result (Arndt, p. 287). It is also possible to regard *epi* as "on the basis of" and to understand Paul's thought as seeing Christ's vicarious death as securing man's freedom from the divine penalty, and on the basis of this freedom, salvation had been offered.

enslavement to sin and its penalty (John 8:34-36), and from their servitude to any religious system of law, whether Mosaic (Gal. 3:13) or pagan (Gal. 4:8-9). The emphatic use of the Greek pronoun for "you" (humeis) and the designation of the readers as "brethren" stresses the confidence Paul has that the Galatians have truly been set free in Christ.

This freedom, however, must not provide an opportunity for the flesh to assert itself in opposition to the will of God. The word "occasion"[2] (KJV) means a starting point, opportunity, or pretext.[3] It can denote the base of operations for an expedition.[4] Here the "flesh" is regarded as the enemy which may conceivably use this Christian "freedom" from the restraints of law to begin a campaign of sinful indulgence.

"Flesh" is frequently Paul's term to describe what man is apart from God. It is not merely a reference to the physical substance of a human being, but includes also his thoughts and aspirations. It is "the product of natural generation apart from the morally transforming power of the Spirit of God; all that comes to a man by inheritance rather than from the operation of the divine Spirit."[5] Inasmuch as all men since the Fall are sinners, man's "flesh" is sinful, always tending toward sin and unable to achieve the righteousness God requires. Even Christians are still "in the flesh" (2:20), but are not to live "after the flesh" (II Cor. 10:3). The "flesh" never improves; hence it must not be given a starting point or it will bring spiritual ruin.

In a striking paradox, Paul states that believers should use their freedom to engage in serving one another. The verb "serve" could be translated "be slaving for" (douleuete), and it denotes a continual serving of others, just as a slave must carry out his responsibilities to his master. Paul can be understood as saying to those who are so enamored with servitude to the Mosaic Law that they should devote themselves rather to serving the needs of others. The key is found in Christian "love," produced by the

---

[2]Greek: aphormēn.

[3]Georg Bertram, "Aphormē," TDNT, 5, 472-74.

[4]Arndt, p. 127.

[5]E. D. Burton, A Critical and Exegetical Commentary on the Epistle to the Galatians (Edinburgh, reprint ed., 1971), p. 493.

indwelling Spirit rather than by the outward compulsion of a legal system.

VERSE 14. It is by the exercise of this love which always seeks the welfare of its object that "all the law is fulfilled." Paul quotes Leviticus 19:18, "Thou shalt love thy neighbor as thyself." In its original context, "neighbor" referred to fellow Jews. However, Jesus taught that one's neighbor is anyone whom he can help (Luke 10:25-37). He used the same Old Testament passage for summarizing the second table of the law (Matt. 22:39). Of course, the second table was based on the first and cannot be accomplished apart from it (Matt. 22:36-40). Men's relations with their fellows can only be correct if first their relation to God is proper. Regeneration by faith produces within the heart a love which desires to accomplish the very things that the law specified but could not produce. This love also prevents license, and leaves the believer a free man who willingly serves the good of others.

VERSE 15. The bickering which was presently going on in Galatia could only result in the extinction of their churches. "Bite," "devour," and "consume" depict the law of the jungle whereby wild animals prey on one another and reduce their numbers accordingly. In a similar manner, freedom from the restraints of the law without Christian love in the heart can easily lead to lawless conduct which is devastating to spiritual life. The form of the statement[6] suggests that this condition was actually occurring in Galatia. That such language was no exaggeration can be seen from the similar situation confronting Paul at Antioch as he wrote this epistle (Acts 15:1-2). Whenever any teaching which questions the basis on which men are saved is injected into the church, turmoil is inevitable. Doubts, recrimination, vilification, slanders, misrepresentations, and disillusionment soon attach themselves to the legitimate concern for doctrinal soundness, and it is not long until the real issues become obscured. One is reminded of the appropriateness of Luke's description of a similar result in another setting: "Some therefore cried one thing, and some another: for the assembly was confused: and the more part knew not wherefore they were

---

[6]A first class condition using *ei* with indicative verbs.

come together!" (Acts 19:32). Many a local church has ceased to be effective for God because Christian liberty has been accompanied by selfish license rather than by love for others.

2. The obligation to walk by the Spirit (5:16)

VERSE 16. Walking is often used by Paul as a metaphor for daily living since it so aptly suggests the progressive round of activities which comprise the routine of life (Rom. 6:4; 8:4; 13:13; 14:15). Here the Holy Spirit is named as the agent[7] who desires to regulate the believer's walk. This is the meaning of another New Testament expression, "filled with the Spirit" (cf. Eph. 5:18). When the believer submits his will to the control of the Holy Spirit instead of to the desires of his fleshly nature, his walk will be in the true liberty of the sons of God. It will "not at all carry out the desire of the flesh." The negative is emphatic in the original text.[8] The two procedures are opposites. If one is controlled by the Holy Spirit, he will of necessity be proceeding in a direction away from the sinful desires of the flesh.

Some have regarded pneuma in this verse as a reference to the human spirit rather than the Holy Spirit,[9] largely on the supposition that flesh and spirit form a better pair of opposites than flesh and the Holy Spirit. However, a closer examination reveals that flesh and spirit are not true opposites, for the human spirit is part of the flesh (note the list of flesh sins in 5:19-21). The only way to make them opposites is to treat "spirit" as the regenerated spirit of man and then the Holy Spirit has been brought into the picture. It is preferable, therefore, to regard the contrast as between the old nature of man ("flesh") and the new nature controlled by the Holy Spirit.

3. The conflict between the flesh and the Spirit (5:17-24)

VERSE 17. The flesh and the Holy Spirit have contrary desires for man. What man is naturally as a result of the Fall (i.e., the

---

[7]Pneumati is an instrumental of agency. H. C. Dana and J. R. Mantey, *A Manual Grammar of the Greek New Testament* (New York, 1946), p. 91.

[8]Greek: ou mē.

[9]For example, R. C. H. Lenski, *Interpretation of St. Paul's Epistles to the Galatians, to the Ephesians, and to the Philippians* (Columbus, 1946) pp. 280-83.

flesh) is in constant opposition to the purposes of God. Not merely are the grosser sensual sins in view but all thoughts and deeds which proceed from fallen man (5:19-21). In contrast the Holy Spirit indwelling each believer continually seeks to cause a walking in the will of God. The believer possesses the Spirit, but he is also still in the flesh (Gal. 2:20). Consequently there is conflict because these are opposing principles.

The result[10] is that the Christian is often not doing what in his heart he desires. "So that whatever you may wish, these things you are not doing" (literal). The thought is similar to Paul's lament in Romans 7:15ff. "For what I would, that do I not; but what I hate, that do I." Christian consciences often disapprove. Actions frequently fall short of good intentions.[11]

VERSE 18. The answer, however, is not that the Christian has been placed under the law. On the contrary, the law had guarded men until the coming of Christ (3:24), but Christ has set believers free from the law (3:25; 5:1). They are not under its penalty because Christ paid it in full as their substitute. They are not under its jurisdiction because it has been annulled (Heb. 7:12, 18). Nor are believers in violation of its spiritual intent; for as they walk in love by the enabling power of the Spirit, they are actually fulfilling the law (5:13-14).

VERSE 19. Continual practicing of the deeds of the flesh shows that one's old nature has not changed, and this disqualifies from participation in God's kingdom. No one should plead ignorance of what the works of the flesh are, for they are well known and public. Paul does not claim that his list is exhaustive, but it is representative (hatina, "of which kind"). This dismal recital will be followed by a contrasting enumeration of fruit produced by the Holy Spirit. "Works" is an apt designation of these productions of the natural man, for they are the result of natural human activity unaided by the Spirit of God.

The first three works of the flesh denote evils in the realm of

---

[10]The use of hina to indicate result is well established, although it is not as common as its use in purpose clauses. See Arndt, p. 378.

[11]An alternate view regards hina as indicating purpose. The statement is understood to mean that when the believer wants to follow the Spirit, the flesh opposes; and when he wishes to follow the flesh, the Spirit opposes. In either instance he is frustrated from doing what he wants.

sensuality, particularly relating to sex.[12] Fornication (*porneia*)
is the general term for sexual immorality. A cognate word *pornē*
meant "prostitute," and may be derived from *pernēmi*, meaning
to sell. The word-family is thus influenced by the thought of sex
which is sold. Greek and Roman life was permeated with extra-
marital sex, often under a religious guise. William Barclay has
observed that "chastity was the one completely new virtue
which Christianity introduced into the pagan world."[13] It is
small wonder, therefore, that it faced obstacles to overcome.

"Uncleanness" (*akatharsia*) can denote physical dirt, ceremonial impurity, or moral defilement. It describes what is soiled
and repulsive. In its ceremonial use, it denotes that which sepa-
rates people from God. It is broader than mere sexual evil, but it
can denote impure thoughts and associations which can eventually lead to immoral acts.

"Wantonness" is an appropriate translation for the third term
(*aselgeia*). In two other Pauline listings it is grouped among
sexual sins (Rom. 13:13; II Cor. 12:21), and this obviously is the
case here. Barclay has traced the term in numerous Hellenistic
and Roman writers, and found the essence of it as outrageous
behavior, totally indifferent to public decency.[14]

VERSE 20. The next two words describe vices involving false
religion. "Idolatry" (*eidōlolatria*), the worship of false gods and
their idols, was often associated with sexual immorality. Hence
the transition to this section of Paul's list was a natural one.
Sacred prostitutes were often attached to pagan temples, and
idolatry frequently involved immorality as part of their worship.
"Witchcraft" (*pharmakeia*) refers to the practice of magic or
sorcery. The term originally meant medical treatment with
drugs (cf. the English "pharmacy"), but it developed the meaning of witchcraft because sorcerers often used potions in practicing their evil art. At Ephesus the gospel preached by Paul caused
many sorcerers to become Christians and abandon their former
deeds in a public renunciation (Acts 19:19).

The next eight vices refer to personal animosities. "Hatreds"

---

[12]The first term in the KJV listing ("adultery") has poor manuscript support and
should be dropped.

[13]William Barclay, *Flesh and Spirit* (Nashville, 1962), p. 27.

[14] Ibid., p. 32.

Fig. 14. The Mound of Derbe (Kerti Hüyük), fourth of the Galatian cities visited by Paul. *Burdick*

(*echthrai*) is plural, and denotes hostile feelings and actions which the flesh harbors and gives vent to. The term describes the attitude existing when men are enemies (*echthroi*). "Strife" (*eris*) is the quarrelling and contention that results from a condition of enmity and hatred. It was characteristic of the church at Corinth when it split into parties and bickered within its ranks (I Cor. 1:11; 3:3; II Cor. 12:20). "Jealousy" (*zēlos;* KJV "emulations") is a term which can have the good sense of "zeal" or "ardor" (Rom. 10:2), but it is capable of degenerating into its negative meaning. It here suggests an attitude of rivalry and concern for personal advancement.

"Outbursts of anger" (*thumoi;* KJV "wrath") uses a plural to depict repeated displays of animosity, in contrast to the more settled states represented by its Greek synonym *orgē* ("wrath"). "Displays of selfishness" (*eritheiai*) is a translation which fits well all of the New Testament occurrences of this term (note specially Phil. 1:17; 2:3; James 3:14, 16). It is derived from the word for day-laborer (*erithos*), and the unfavorable sense of working only for one's own interests, in contrast to one who donates his service in philanthropic activity. Evil jealousy is always selfish, and anger often is.

"Divisions" (dichostasiai; KJV "seditions") are the dissensions and splits which are the inevitable result when personal conflicts run their course. A factious spirit eventually results in a splintering of whatever group has existed. "Parties" (haireseis; KJV "heresies") are the groups which emerge when the divisions noted above take on distinct identities. The term did not necessarily denote what we call a heretical sect, but simply a group of persons who shared a particular belief. Later the term came to be applied to beliefs which were unorthodox. In the present context the emphasis is on the divisiveness of such parties.

VERSE 21. The last of the eight terms denoting personal animosities is "envyings" (phthonoi). It is allied in thought with "jealousy," but is the more serious of the two. Jealousy can have a good sense, but it is also used of a selfish rivalry. If it is unchecked it can easily lead to envy. "Zēlos [jealousy], we might say, is the envy which casts grudging looks; phthonos [envying] is the envying which has arrived at hostile deeds."[15]

The last two items designate evil practices associated with drunkenness.[16] "Drunkenness" (methai) and "revellings" (kōmoi) are used together also in Romans 13:13. They describe the evils of intoxication and the carousings which are so frequently associated with drinking. The drunken celebrations depicted by these terms were often accompanied by idolatry and immoral practices. All sorts of evils could be perpetrated when men gave up their self-control under the influence of drink.

The reference to this dismal list as "such things" indicates that the listing was representative and not exhaustive. The above are not the only evil works of which the flesh is capable. However, the listing was sufficiently broad to illustrate Paul's point that those who habitually practice[17] such deeds as these will not inherit the kingdom of God. This sort of conduct is

---

[15]Ibid., p. 47.

[16]The textual support for "murders" (KJV) is weak, and the word has not been included in ASV, NASB, or NIV.

[17]The Greek expression is hoi . . . prassontes, a present participle conveying the idea of continuing an unbroken practice.

characteristic, to a greater or lesser degree, of unsaved persons, ones who are limited to "the flesh" as their sphere of action. The continual exhibition of these works is evidence of the unregenerate nature undisturbed by the Spirit. Christians, it is true, may fall into some of the sins mentioned here when they fail to walk by the Spirit, for they still have an old nature which sometimes entices persuasively, but such will not be the general pattern of their lives.

VERSE 22. The fruit produced by the Holy Spirit stands in sharpest contrast to the sordid and damaging works of the flesh. Even the choice of the term "fruit," rather than retention of the parallelism by using "works of the Spirit," is appropriate because the nine elements to be named are a unity and are the product of spiritual growth, not something which man can do, in contrast to the unorganized and irrational excesses of the flesh.

"Love" (*agapē*) stands first in the list, and it receives this emphasis elsewhere in Paul (I Cor. 13). This is the virtue produced within the believer by the Spirit of God which far transcends mere earthly emotions. From the use of the noun and the corresponding verb in the New Testament, the particular meaning becomes clearer. This love is a characteristic of God (I John 4:8). When it is performed by men, it fulfills the law (Rom. 13:10). It always seeks the highest good of its object and does not cease or change, even when it is rebuffed. When produced by the Spirit, it enables the believer to love God and his fellows in the most exalted of ways.

"Joy" (*chara*) is that Spirit-produced virtue which enables the believer to rejoice in all the circumstances of life. Even in trials, the believer may retain the joy of the Lord which prevents his giving way to total despair. This is the only occurrence of the word "joy" in Galatians, but the New Testament is filled with the concept.

"Peace" (*eirēnē*) refers here to the peace supplied by the Spirit to encourage and stabilize the heart of the believer (Phil. 4:7). There is another kind of peace, the "peace of God," described in the New Testament which refers to the cessation of hostility between the sinner and God. This is received in justification (Rom. 5:1). The peace which is a fruit of the Spirit is the tranquility which is ministered to the believer daily to sustain him during his Christian life.

"Longsuffering" (makrothumia) and the next two terms are qualities which appear in our relations with others. Longsuffering is that virtue in which a person keeps himself under control for a long time. He does not retaliate nor lash out in frustration. He displays a characteristic of Christ who is longsuffering toward sinners (I Tim. 1:16).

"Kindness" (chrēstotēs; KJV "gentleness") is a term used frequently of God to denote His gracious attitude and acts toward sinners (Rom. 2:4; Eph. 2:7; Titus 3:4). The Holy Spirit produces in the believer a corresponding attitude whereby he puts love into action and in so doing he demonstrates the character of God whose image he bears.

"Goodness" (agathosunē) is a term occurring only four times in the New Testament (cf. Rom. 15:14; Eph. 5:9; II Thess. 1:11). It is related to agathos, a very common word for "good." The word denotes moral excellence in operation. The term is a broad one and can also indicate generosity.[18]

"Faith" (pistis) is that quality which a person displays when he trusts God. This characteristic is not merely to be exercised at the time of repentance and conversion, but should be increasingly displayed as one walks with God each day. The word can also be used with the meaning of faithfulness or reliability.

VERSE 23. "Meekness" (prautēs) translates a word for which no exact equivalent exists in English. The term combines strength and gentleness. It denotes strength that is under control. Moses was the meekest man on the earth in his day (Num. 12:3). Although he was capable of great anger when it was necessary, he was also submissive to God and kept his temper in check under trying circumstances. Meekness was also a characteristic of Jesus Christ (Matt. 11:29), who had the strength to deliver the severest denunciations, but the gentleness to welcome little children and to minister to the sinful and suffering.

"Self-control" (enkrateia; KJV "temperance") denotes the ability to hold oneself in check, to be in control. It describes self-restraint, self-discipline, and chastity. In contrast to the

---

[18]Arndt, p. 3.

works of the flesh just named, self-control can be understood as the spiritual opposite to the excesses of sensualism, particularly in sexual matters, drinking, and temperament. The reference, however, is broad enough to cover all areas where self-discipline is required.

"Against such" indicates that there is other fruitage[19] of the Spirit, in addition to the nine items mentioned here. These are simply representative. Those who exhibit this sort of life find no law poised against them. Their lives will be pleasing to God. Paul's point, however, is that this sort of pleasing conduct does not come about by placing people under the law, but by walking by the power of the Spirit.

VERSE 24. "Those who belong to Christ Jesus" (NASB) are true Christians. As such they all possess the Holy Spirit (Rom. 8:9) and should be displaying the fruits of the Spirit, rather than indulging in the works of the flesh. True Christians have "crucified the flesh." At conversion the believer made a radical break with the past. By accepting God's verdict on sin and receiving by faith Christ's work on his behalf, the sinner identified himself with Christ, and his fleshly nature was in effect nailed to the cross. Of course, the old nature can still harass him because until glorification occurs at death or at the Lord's return the old nature still exists within the believer, but officially it has been crucified and has no more authority over the Christian. Elsewhere Paul urges Christians to "reckon" themselves dead to sin (Rom. 6:11). It is only when we fail to listen to the Spirit and instead heed the stirrings of the old "passions and desires" (NASB) that we fall into the works of the flesh.

4. The encouragement to consistency (5:25-26)

VERSE 25. In concluding this impressive passage on the Christian life, Paul urges the Galatians to conduct themselves in harmony with the Spirit who has granted them life. "If we live by the Spirit, let us keep in line with the Spirit." He is exhorting his readers to make sure that their lives are consistent with their

---

[19]"Such" (*tōn toioutōn*) could refer to "such persons," rather than "such fruit." However, the result is not materially different, for the fruit is understood as being developed in persons.

new position as sons of God by the Spirit. "If we live" is a kind of conditional statement which assumes the condition to be true.[20] The sense is, "If we live by the Spirit, and I assume that you are Christians and therefore have been born again by the Holy Spirit." "Keep in line with" (stoichōmen; KJV "walk") is not the usual word for "walk," but is one which emphasizes belonging to a series, being in a row or rank.[21] It suggests keeping in harmony with some norm or standard (compare another use of the same word in 6:16). Hence, since all believers possess the Holy Spirit (and if anyone does not, he is not a Christian, Rom. 8:9), the way to avoid the sins of the flesh is not to revert to a keeping of the Mosaic Law, but to bring his life into conformity with the will of the Spirit who produces the fruit which pleases God. The Spirit illuminates the Word of God and provides the inner dynamic for a fruitful walk. Paul's statement clearly recognizes the fact that sometimes Christian conduct does not conform to the ideal. The exhortation, therefore, is always in order.

VERSE 26. Negatively stated, the believer's conduct should not become characterized by "empty conceit" (kenodoxoi; KJV "vain glory"). If the Galatian churches had been polarizing themselves into factions over the Judaizing issue, it would have been easy for each group to become conceited and boastful about its own position and to disparage others. Some may have boasted about their liberty from the law and were going too far in "challenging one another" (allēlous prokaloumenoi; KJV "provoking") to be more bold in exercising their new freedom in Christ, perhaps to the point of turning liberty into license. The more conservative among them may have been "envying" their bolder brethren, even though their own consciences would not yet allow them to imitate them. A similar problem is discussed by Paul in Romans 14 and I Corinthians 8, where the weaker and stronger Christians are cautioned against despising or judging one another. The life that is truly Christian is a walk by the Spirit, sensitive to His leading and measured by the standard of

---

[20]A Greek first class condition, utilizing ei with the indicative mood.
[21]Gerhard Dilling, "Stoicheō," TDNT, 7, 666-69.

God's Word. It is not a mechanical conformity to outward codes, nor a lapse into fleshly excesses under the guise of "freedom," but a vibrant living with energy and direction supplied by the Holy Spirit who dwells within.

Questions for Discussion

1. What is the "freedom" to which Christians have been called?
2. How can a Christian prevent his liberty from degenerating into license?
3. What is the "flesh"?
4. Why can't the law produce lives which please God?
5. If all Christians have crucified the flesh, why do they still have conflicts with the flesh?
6. What are some hindrances to the production of spiritual fruit?

Chapter 12

Respond to Others

(Galatians 6:1-10)

As Paul discussed the practical side of the Christian faith, he has shown how believers need to stand firm on the right principle (5:1-12), and to walk by the power and guidance of the Holy Spirit (5:13-26). He now explains what is involved in a walk by the Spirit. It is not some introspective experience which takes no thought of others. On the contrary, each believer is responsible to have a concern for his fellows, and to help in bearing their burdens whether caused by moral faults or temporal needs.

C. Exhortation to Fulfill Responsibilities to Others (6:1-10)

1. *Assist those who are spiritually weak* (6:1-5)

VERSE 1. Although every believer should walk by the Spirit and not yield to the impulses of the flesh, the fact remains that not all do so as consistently as they should. The responsibility rests on those who have not displayed this weakness to strengthen the offending person. Although the offender is here called simply a "man" (*anthropos*), it appears from the context that he is a Christian brother. The emphasis in the passage is on concerns for "one another" in the Christian society.

The case described is of a person who is "overtaken in a fault." The Greek word employed (*prolambanō*) is not used elsewhere in the New Testament with this sense; however, the meaning of "surprise, overtake, or detect" is found in the papyri and LXX (Apoc.).[1] Two views are current regarding the circumstances of the man's being "overtaken." Was he overtaken or surprised by the transgression? If so, the implication may be that it was no deliberate sin but a sudden impulse, and thus it should be

---

[1]Arndt, p. 715

treated more graciously. Or was the man surprised or detected in
the transgression by someone else, and was thus caught "red-
handed"? This understanding stresses the serious nature of the
case, and shows that even such cases are to be dealt with kindly.
KJV suggests the former, and NASB implies the latter. I prefer
the second as being the simpler understanding of the statement.
Strictly speaking, one can be overtaken by temptation but not by
transgression (paraptōmati), for that requires an act of the individual.

"Ye which are spiritual" are obligated to restore the erring
brother. These are believers who are walking by the Spirit (5:25)
and thus are manifesting the fruit of the Spirit in their lives
(5:22-23), rather than displaying the works of the flesh exhibited
by the brother who has transgressed (5:16-21). Every Christian
should be one of "the spiritual" for all believers have their life
from the Spirit (5:25), but this is not always the case. In this
verse, "the spiritual" are not simply "the Christians," for the
sinning brother is also a Christian. It refers to those Christians
who at this time are spiritually stronger and more mature than
this stumbling brother.

To "restore" (katartizete) is to straighten out the problem,
repair the damage, and thus to equip the offender for renewed
usefulness in the church. The same verb is used in the New
Testament of mending torn or tangled nets (Matt. 4:21; Mark 1:19)
and of equipping the human body or the world to fulfill their
functions (Heb. 10:5; 11:3). It must be done, however, in "the
spirit of meekness," displaying the fact that the restorers are
among "the spiritual" by exhibiting this fruit of the Spirit (5:23).
The previous instruction has employed plurals as the church
has been admonished collectively to restore the offender. Now
Paul shifts to the singular "considering thyself," for this was
something each believer must do individually. Even "the
spiritual" still possess the flesh and each person must look at
himself as well as at the sinner, lest he "also be tempted." There
must not be among "the spiritual" any spiritual pride.

VERSE 2. "Bear ye one another's burdens" should first be
understood in the light of the previous verse. The believer who
is living as he should will be concerned about recovering others
from their moral lapses. In some cases his help must take the

form of restoring the wayward to the path of rectitude. In other instances his alertness may help a brother in times of temptation or other stress and thus enable him to avoid falling into transgression. The burdens imposed by remorse, weakness, spiritual immaturity, and difficult circumstances can be eased by the faithful efforts of a Christian friend. As a principle, however, the injunction can be understood as applicable to every sort of helpfulness in which Christian love can be displayed. In the light of 6:5, Paul's meaning in 6:2 is that believers are to assist their brethren in carrying their burdens, but not to take over the whole burden themselves.

Such brotherly action will "fulfill the law of Christ." Paul refers to the principle of love which fulfills all that the Mosaic Law included in the second table (5:14). Jesus stated the same thing (Matt. 22:39) and called His restatement the "new commandment" whereby the standard for love was to be Christ's love which He had shown toward His followers (John 13:34-35). It is a spiritual fruit (5:22), produced not by the compulsion of an external code but by the transformation of the heart by the Holy Spirit.

VERSE 3. Sometimes pride gets in the way of helping others. This is often the case when the person needing assistance with his burdens has fallen into sin. The person who should be helping must not deceive himself into a "holier-than-thou" attitude, even though he may not be guilty of the same transgression which has entrapped his brother. Pride is likewise sinful, and can easily lead him also into sinful acts (6:1).

Paul is not necessarily saying that everyone is "nothing," although it is true that no one has any basis for self-glory before God. His point, however, is that if a person considers himself to possess great moral strength (in contrast to the brother who has just fallen), when in fact he is really weak also, his confidence is self-delusion. He is himself a likely subject for a serious fall.

VERSE 4. Instead of deceiving oneself by maintaining a superior attitude toward the sinning brother, every Christian should carefully examine the quality of his own conduct. When a person's life measures up to what God expects as revealed by Scripture, then "he will have reason for boasting in regard to himself alone" (NASB). The boasting referred to here means the reason or grounds for boasting (kauchēma), and may be understood in a good sense (as in Phil. 2:16). Legitimate boasting or glorying is the result of valid reasons which stand on their own merits. There is a proper satisfaction which the believer can enjoy from knowing that his life and labors are pleasing to God. But he must make sure that he has evaluated his life by the proper standard. Merely to compare oneself to a stumbling brother and then to feel smugly superior is to use the wrong yardstick. It is like the little boy who proudly announced he was nine feet tall because he had made his own ruler and measured himself. The only valid standard is the Word of God. If one's life conforms to that standard he has grounds for rejoicing, far more than if he has merely pitted his conduct against that of someone else.

VERSE 5. This statement summarizes the previous verse. "For every man shall bear his own burden." The term "burden" (phortion) differs from the one used in 6:2 (barē); and although it is not possible to draw a sharp distinction between them, Paul undoubtedly used a different word in 6:5 to avoid a contradiction with 6:2. The word phortion is used of a burdensome load (Matt. 23:4; Luke 11:46) and of a ship's cargo (Acts 27:10), but also it denotes the easy load which Christ imposes on His followers (Matt. 11:30). By allowing Christ's statement (Matt. 11:28-30) to interpret the meaning for us, we understand Paul's reference to mean the responsibilities of practical discipleship which our Lord expects His followers to accept.[2] This is the "work" (6:4) with which each believer should concern himself. He cannot pass it off to another, nor can he excuse his failures by pointing to the failures of his brethren. He must carry his own load, and at Christ's judgment seat he must answer for his own discipleship.

2. Provide for the needs of teachers (6:6-9)

VERSE 6. This directive is given to those who have received Christian instruction from their leaders. Even in these early days of the church, the local congregations were organized in order for believers to grow in their understanding of God's Word, to

---

[2]Konrad Weiss, "Phortion," TDNT, 9, 85-86.

profit from their fellowship with one another, and to engage in united worship of their Lord.[3] One of the gifts which the ascended Christ gave to His church was the gift of the pastor-teacher (Eph. 4:11). The entire congregation is thus indebted to its spiritual leaders, and is here directed to "communicate to him that teacheth in all good things."

The verb "communicate" *(koinōeitō)* has a broad range of uses in the New Testament. The basic idea of the word-family is "common" or "having in common." It often denoted a fellowship, participation, or sharing with someone. In a religious sense it was used of the participation of believers with Christ and His blessings. The word was also used of the mutual sharing among believers through their common life in Christ. The idea of "having a share in" is not unrelated to the thought of "giving a share to," and thus the latter sense is also found frequently. This meaning of contributing a share is what Paul means here. It is precisely this sense of the verb which he uses in Romans 12:13, "contributing to the needs of the saints." Although it is sometimes objected that "all good things" is too broad to be restricted to finances,[4] there are many places in the New Testament where the expression "good things" is clearly referring to temporal goods (Luke 1:53; 12:18, 19; 16:25).

Furthermore, the obligation of believers to support their teachers financially is a frequent Pauline theme. Note I Corinthians 9:3-14; II Corinthians 11:7-9; Philippians 4:10-19; II Thessalonians 3:7-9; and I Timothy 5:17-18 for other discussions of a similar nature. The illustration of sowing and reaping used in the present discussion (6:7) is used also by Paul in I Corinthians 9:10-11 in a context where financial support is clearly in view.

The mention of this responsibility may have occurred to Paul as a needed caution against misunderstanding his remarks in 6:5. By insisting that each one is responsible for his own load, he did not mean that a concern for others should be discarded, nor that the church had no responsibility for its ministers. All too often, however, an unfortunate episode with one minister is

---

[3]For the organizing of these churches in Galatia, see Acts 14:23.
[4]Frederic Rendall, "The Epistle to the Galatians," *EGT*, 3, 189.

allowed to color the thinking of a congregation toward all ministers, and their feelings are reflected in the way they respond to
the matter Paul raised in 6:6. Martin Luther noted this same sad
practice of many Christians in his day:

> In the old days when the Pope reigned supreme everybody
> paid plenty for masses. The begging friars brought in their
> share. Commercial priests counted the daily offerings. From
> these extortions our countrymen are now delivered by the
> Gospel. You would think they would be grateful for their
> emancipation and give generously for the support of the
> ministry of the Gospel and the relief of impoverished Chris-
> tians. Instead, they rob Christ. When the members of a Chris-
> tian congregation permit their pastor to struggle along in pen-
> ury, they are worse than heathen.[5]

VERSE 7. As Paul thought of this tendency in his day to treat
their godly ministers in a niggardly and demeaning fashion
(while perhaps lavishing attention and material benefits on the
ear-tickling teachers of falsehood), he reminded the Galatians of
the seriousness of these matters. Their Christian lives were in
full view of God, and "God is not mocked." That is, God cannot
be mocked without incurring His displeasure and discipline.
"Mocked" (*muktērizetai*) comes from the word for "nose," and
means "to turn up one's nose" or "treat contemptuously." To
claim that one accepts the whole counsel of God as found in His
Word and then to act in contradiction to what the Word commands so clearly is to treat God with contempt.

"For whatsoever a man soweth that shall he also reap" is a
principle which relates results to causes. The same metaphor is
used in I Corinthians 9:10-11 regarding the right of ministers to
receive appropriate compensation. Paul used it again in
II Corinthians 9:6 regarding giving of money to the Lord's work.
In the present passage the Galatians are warned that if they deal
meagerly with their minister, they can expect to suffer barrenness in their own lives.

VERSE 8. From the mention that the harvest is dependent on
the nature of the seed that is sown, Paul proceeds to describe the
two contrasting kinds of crops. "He that soweth to his flesh"

---

[5]Martin Luther, *A Commentary on St. Paul's Epistle to the Galatians*, trans.
Theodore Graebner (Grand Rapids, n.d.), pp. 243-44.

Fig. 15. Harvest scene in the hills of Ephraim. *Levant*.

(literally, "to his own flesh") describes the person who invests his life (and specially here, his money) for the gratification of his fleshly nature. The apostle has previously discussed the problem of the flesh which is possessed by every person and which continually moves in opposition to the Spirit of God (5:13-26). The inevitable harvest that comes from pandering to every desire of the natural man is "corruption." The concept of "corruption" or "decay" was used of physical destruction (Rom. 8:21; I Cor. 15:42; Col. 2:22), and sometimes with the idea of man's susceptibility to death (II Cor. 4:16). Thus it is found in contrast to "eternal life" as here. What is merely earthly and sensual is doomed to eventual decay, and in the moral and immaterial realm, to eternal destruction.

In contrast, "he that soweth to the Spirit" is the one who invests in areas prompted by the Holy Spirit, such as involvement in supporting God's work and His ministers. In Paul's view, refusal to have a share in spiritual enterprises meant that one preferred to use his goods for his own selfish ends. He would not be walking by the Spirit, but by the flesh. To encourage his readers the apostle lifts their eyes to the future consummation of their salvation by reminding them that sowing to the Spirit will bring the harvest of life everlasting. At Christ's return believers will receive glorified bodies no longer subject to fleshly passions and death.

VERSE 9. The ever-present danger is that believers may "grow weary" or "lose heart" (NASB) while engaged in doing what is good because they do not see immediate results from their efforts. Paul uses similar language in II Thessalonians 3:13. The wording describes laborers in the harvest field who may cease their efforts after prolonged labor, or may faint from exposure to the weather. They are reminded that "in due season" the harvest will come. Generous acts toward others do not always bring instantaneous commendation. At times Christians may suffer rather than prosper after doing good (I Peter 2:20). They must remember that the reaping of the spiritual harvest comes when God determines that the time is right.

The promise is clear that reaping will be enjoyed "if we faint not."[6] The same word (*ekluomai*) was used by Jesus in the

---

[6]The participle is used here conditionally.

physical sense of fainting from lack of food (Matt. 15:32; Mark 8:3). Its use here is of spiritual weariness and collapse (as in Heb. 12:3, 5). The final harvest and reward will come at Christ's return when every believer's works will be examined. Each one should pursue his Christian life by "sowing" in the Spirit's power and trusting God for the harvest.

3. Do good to all men, and particularly to other Christians (6:10)

VERSE 10. The principle of investing one's life ("sowing") in areas prompted by the Spirit rather than the flesh has been applied in the foregoing section to providing for one's spiritual teachers, but it is by no means limited to this. There are countless opportunities to display one's Christian faith by appropriate deeds. Therefore, "as we have . . . opportunity," the situation should be grasped to "work what is good toward all men" (literal). The word "opportunity" (kairon) is the same one which was translated "season" in 6:9. There is a season for sowing just as for reaping, and that season is now. Thus Paul has enlarged his earlier reference to financial assistance for teachers to include all sorts of good deeds for all men.

There is a special sense, however, in which believers are responsible for others like themselves who have by faith become part of the household of God (Eph. 2:19). This recognition of their spiritual union with each other because of their oneness in Christ caused the early church from the beginning to share their goods with one another and to be concerned about their brothers in Christ in all ways. In times of material need they pooled their resources (Acts 2:44-45; 4:34-35; 11:27-30). When suffering came, they ministered in prayer and in personal ways (Acts 12:5; II Tim. 1:16-18). It is a Biblical principle that members of one family have a special responsibility for one another (I Tim. 5:8), and this is also true when the family is the spiritual one of the household of God.

Questions for Discussion

1. Who are "the spiritual"?
2. What are some ways that Christians can restore a sinning brother?

3. Who comprise the household of faith?
4. What are some cases where the "sowing and reaping" principle was demonstrated in your experience?
5. Can you think of cases where the "sowing and reaping" principle has been misapplied?
6. Should believers support charitable organizations that are not Christian?

Chapter 13

Concluding Summary

(Galatians 6:11-18)

The composing of the Epistle to the Galatians must have put great strain on the apostle Paul. As he considered all the circumstances, it was clear that no mere communication of pleasantries would meet the needs of the Galatians. Their situation was disturbed and the danger was real. The issues involved were crucial, and halfway measures would not be good enough. Matters must be confronted which affected men's convictions, their traditions, and their emotional attachments. It was important, therefore, to deal with the problems in a way that would produce a sympathetic and favorable response.

At the same time, Paul himself was emotionally involved in the issues at hand. He had founded the churches of Galatia. It was his teaching which the Judaizers were undermining. His authority as an apostle was under attack. How could he preserve the work he had so recently founded when he must counteract his foes from a distance?

That Paul had done a masterful job of stating his case and demonstrating its rightness was obvious to the discerning reader. The ending of the letter would be the key to its effectiveness. The author must end on the right note if he wished the readers to adopt his views and put them into practice. The letter has made some harsh charges. Somehow Paul must leave the impression that his explanations are for their good. He must convey the thought that these arguments were not just theological bickering, or the jealous complaints of a leader who was about to lose his following. On the contrary, they were the product of a deep concern by their spiritual father.

The writer also needed to make it clear that the letter was a genuine product of the apostle. Forgeries were not unknown, and religious counterfeiting was a problem which Paul faced elsewhere in his career (II Thess. 2:2). The final eight verses of

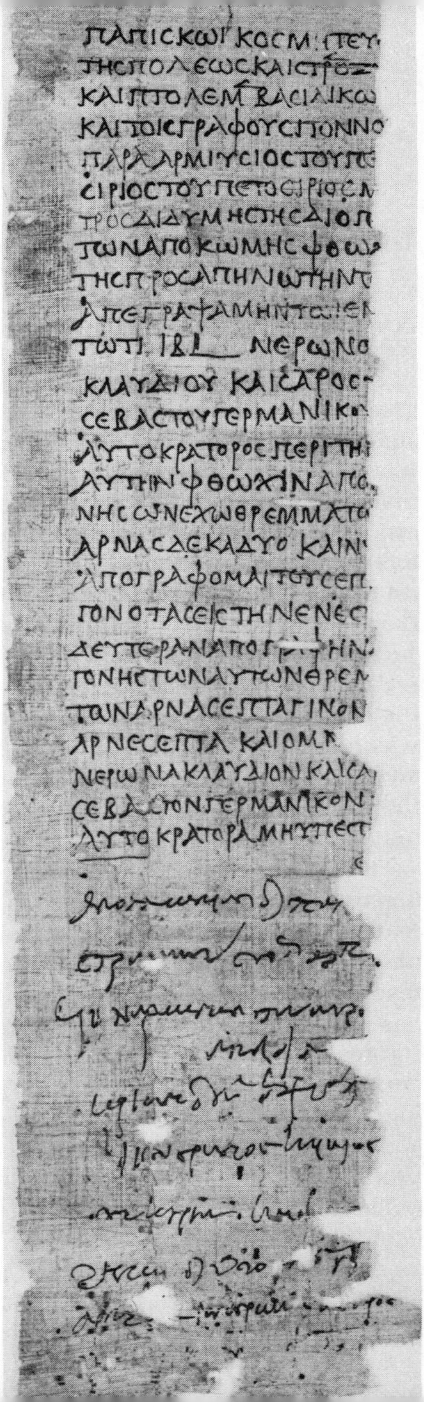

Fig. 16. A first-century papyrus letter, with the main text written in one hand, and an attesting signature with remarks in another hand. *Cambridge*

the epistle show how Paul brought this important discussion to
its conclusion.

A. Authentication of the Epistle (6:11)

VERSE 11. This concluding paragraph was apparently penned
by the apostle himself, and he calls attention to the larger letters
he has used in distinction from the script of the amanuensis who
had written the body of the letter. The services of a scribe to write
the main portion of Paul's letters formed his usual practice (e.g.,
Rom. 16:22), but the apostle authenticated each letter by a few
words in his own handwriting at the end[1] (I Cor. 16:21; Col.
4:18; II Thess. 3:17). This procedure was not only Paul's usual
method, but has been illustrated by the discovery of ancient
papyrus letters showing the same practice (see Fig. 16).

"With what large letters" (pēlikois . . . grammasin) is vastly
preferable to the rendering "how large a letter" (KJV) for several
reasons. The epistle is not unusually long. Furthermore, one
would expect an accusative ("a large letter") rather than a dative
("with what large letters") if the entire document were meant.
Also Paul used the term epistolē rather than grammata for his
written communications. The reference is thus to the larger
letters in Paul's handwriting than those used by the scribe in the
rest of the document. Perhaps the scribe had used the common
cursive script,[2] but Paul wrote his concluding remarks in the
large separately formed uncial letters.

Why did Paul use larger letters at this point? The text gives no
answer, and the suggestions of others are varied but inconclu-
sive. It has been supposed that he had bad eyesight,[3] that he had
a crippled hand from his stoning at Lystra,[4] or that he was not
proficient in writing Greek or at least not as skillful as a pro-

---

[1]The aorist egrapsa (KJV "I have written"; NASB "I am writing") should be
regarded as epistolary. To insist as some do that the aorist must be historical and
then to build an argument on it that Paul penned the entire epistle himself is to
argue from a premise that is less than conclusive. The interpretation given
above is consistent with Paul's stated practice.

[2]Frederic G. Kenyon, Handbook to the Textual Criticism of the New Testament
(Grand Rapids, reprint ed.1953), p. 30.

[3]Frederic Rendall, "The Epistle to the Galatians," EGT, 3, 190.

[4]R. C. H. Lenski, Interpretation of St. Paul's Epistles to the Galatians, to the
Ephesians, and to the Philippians (Columbus, 1946), pp. 312-13.

fessional scribe.[5] Perhaps a better suggestion is that he merely wanted to distinguish his own handwriting from the scribal hand. If so, the emphasis in the sentence should fall on "with my own hand," rather than on "with what large letters." It is also possible that Paul used this device to emphasize the forcefulness of his personal convictions regarding these matters.[6]

B. Final Warning Against the Judaizers (6:12-17)

VERSE 12. In summarizing the major thrust of the epistle, Paul in a few concise statements lays his case on the line. He characterizes the Judaizers as ones who "desire to make a good showing in the flesh" (NASB). The verb used here (euprosōpēsai) was formerly thought to have been unknown prior to the New Testament (and this is its lone New Testament occurrence), but now it has been found in a papyrus letter from 114 B.C.[7] It has the meaning there as here of winning the good opinion of one's neighbors.[8] The Judaizers' concern, however, was exercised "in the flesh." They were doubtless claiming to be Christian believers, but were walking in the flesh and sowing to the flesh (6:6; cf. 5:16), rather than walking by the Spirit.

The Judaizers were attempting[9] to force circumcision on the Gentile converts in Galatia. Their real reason was to gain popularity ("a good showing") and escape persecution "for[10] the cross of Christ." Non-Christian Jews had persistently persecuted Christians, and this had increased as Paul's ministry extended the gospel freely to Gentiles. By insisting on circumcision, Judaizers sought to allay the fears and hatred of their Jewish countrymen and thus escape such persecution as Paul fre-

---

[5]R. A. Cole, *The Epistle of Paul to the Galatians* (Grand Rapids, 1965), p. 180.

[6]J. B. Lightfoot, *The Epistle of St. Paul to the Galatians* (Grand Rapids, reprint ed.), p. 221.

[7]Eduard Lohse, "Euprosōpeō," *TDNT*, 6, 779.

[8]Adolf Deissman, *Light from the Ancient East* (Grand Rapids, reprint ed., 1965), pp. 98-99.

[9]The verb *anangkazousin* (constrain, compel) is a conative present, describing attempted action. The epistle does not imply that the attempt had been successful.

[10]The phrase *tōi staurōi tou Christou* is a dative or instrumental of cause. H. E. Dana and J. R. Mantey, *A Manual Grammar of the Greek New Testament* (New York, 1946), p. 89.

quently encountered from fanatical Jews. They apparently thought that Christianity might be tolerated as simply another Jewish sect if the cross of Christ was not preached as the sole means of man's redemption without the imposition of Mosaic ritual.

VERSE 13. In spite of their strenuous insistence on the rite of circumcision (that is, of requiring Gentile followers of Christ to become full Jewish proselytes as well), the Judaizers are charged by Paul with hypocrisy. These men, says Paul, "do not even keep the Law themselves" (NASB). Inasmuch as Paul attaches obvious blame to them for this, he must mean more than that they did not keep it perfectly (a circumstance which is true of everyone, 3:10). Probably he refers to the fact that they picked out certain features to observe and ignored the rest (like the Jews denounced by Jesus, Luke 11:42, 46). They did not keep any of the law with the motive of heart which God requires. Paul tells his readers what the Judaizers' real motives were: to avoid persecution (6:12) and to boast in their success in winning proselytes (6:13). They wanted to "glory in your flesh." By forcing Gentile Christians to submit to this Jewish rite, they could boast in the number of victories they had won. "Your" (humeterāi) is an emphasized word in the sentence. They would be boasting at your expense. Their interests were strictly external and superficial. Although what the Judaizers were doing involved theological error, there is still a lesson here for all Christians to heed. Boasting about numbers can be merely a desire for a "good showing in the flesh." Certainly it is proper to thank God for spiritual victories that are won, but it is all too easy to boast in numbers and to forget what really counts.

VERSE 14. Paul, however, refused to do his glorying in other than essential matters. For the third time in this epistle[11] he uses the strong disclaimer "may it never be" (mē genoito; KJV "God forbid") to state his own policy. He wants no personal boasting, but intends to do his glorying in relation to the cross of Christ. The cross, of course, is a symbol of Christ's death and its results. At the cross the penalty resultant from God's broken law was paid in full, and all the blessings of salvation were made possi-

---

[11]Galatians 2:17; 3:21; 6:14.

ble. The cross—which normally stood for a hideous form of execution—had become for Paul a symbol of triumph.

When Paul came to understand the gospel and recognize the real meaning of Christ's death on the cross, he found that the world no longer held its former attraction for him. Christ's death had satisfied God's righteousness. Salvation for men was by faith in Christ and His merits, not by any human works or law-keeping. Hence his pride in his Jewish attainments and his rising stature in the world were replaced by trust in the Lord Jesus Christ (Phil. 3:4-9). By identification with Christ in His death and resurrection, Paul had come to experience newness of life whereby the old life that was influenced and controlled by the world was gone (Rom. 6:4).

Similarly, Paul had been crucified so far as the world was concerned. By identifying himself with the crucified Jesus, he was despised with the same disdain as his Master. Paul gave no credit to the world for his spiritual life, and he expected no admiration from it in return. All the glory belonged to Christ.

VERSE 15. The reason why Paul lives by the principle of verse 14 is stated in verse 15. Neither "circumcision," so proudly practiced by Jews and insisted on by Judaizers, nor "uncircumcision," the usual condition of Gentiles, has any relevance to the issue at hand. He has made a similar statement in 5:6. Circumcision offers no spiritual advantage (or disadvantage), and neither does the lack of it. The important thing is the new creation, in which regeneration by the Spirit makes the believer a "new creature" in Christ (II Cor. 5:17). This new condition comes by faith in the One who died on the cross as the sinner's substitute. Works, rites, ceremonies, feast days—all are irrelevant. The new birth comes to those who believe in Christ alone (John 3:3, 5, 16).

VERSE 16. "Walk" is the word "keep in line with" (stoichēsousin), and the clause can be rendered "as many as keep in line with this rule." He refers to the control of conduct by the indwelling Holy Spirit, rather than by a pursuing of the Mosaic Code (5:16, 18, 25). Such a principle of life is possible by God's new creation, whereby the believer in Christ has become a new creature. On such Paul pronounces the dual blessing of peace

and mercy to stabilize and encourage the hearts of God's people
" and relieve them in times of distress.

The phrase "and upon the Israel of God" has been understood
in at least two ways, and each is grammatically possible. Some
understand *kai* as meaning "even," and regard the phrase as an
explanation of the previous "as many as." The reference would
be to the whole Christian community who are sons of Abraham
by faith (3:7, 29), and the phrase would be rendered, "even upon
the Israel of God."

The other view regards the phrase as a singling out of Jewish
Christians for special mention. Having been dealing primarily
with the problem of Gentiles who were being pressured to adopt
Judaistic practices, Paul has just pronounced his approval and
blessing on those who resist that pressure and walk by the
proper rule of Christian conduct. However, he does not wish to
exclude any true Christians from his benediction, so he makes
the additional mention of "the Israel of God," that is, Jews who
were not merely racial descendants of Abraham but were also
sharers of his faith. Paul makes this same distinction elsewhere
between spiritual and mere physical relationship to Abraham
(Rom. 2:28-29; 9:6ff.). Favoring this view is the fact that all of
Paul's other uses of "Israel" or "Israelite" are of the Jewish
nation. Jewish Christian readers might well recognize the concept of "peace upon Israel" as an echo of Psalms 125:5 and 128:6.

VERSE 17. "From henceforth let no man trouble me." Paul had
argued his case well and expected no further outbreak of the
problem in Galatia. He had begun this epistle by stating his
apostolic authority, and now he closes it with an order that no
more troubles of this sort should be imposed on him by these
churches. In fact there is no Scriptural indication that the problem of legalism was ever reopened in Galatia; so there is reason
to understand that Paul's masterful treatise settled the problem
and silenced the opposition.

The readers should have no hesitation in accepting Paul's
apostolic authority, for not only had he demonstrated his
apostleship in chapters 1 and 2, but he also bore in his body "the
marks of Jesus" (*ta stigmata tou lēsou*). In the Greco-Roman
world the word *stigma* referred to a brand mark, and was found

on domestic cattle, deserters from the army, criminals, and
slaves who had been caught after running away, stealing, or
committing some other flagrant offense. The brand was a per-
manent disfigurement placed usually on the body's forehead or
hand (hoof).[12] Paul, however, undoubtedly refers to the physical
scars which he carried as a result of his Christian labors. The
scars from the recent stoning at Lystra were one example (Acts
14:19). The argument is not unlike the response of Antipater, the
father of Herod the Great, when he was accused of disloyalty to
Caesar. Throwing off his garments and exposing his countless
scars, he said he needed to say nothing about his loyalty because
his body shouted it aloud without his saying a word.[13] Were the
Judaizers glorying in their ritual marks and gashes (circumcision)? Then Paul can claim something better—an identification with Jesus even to the sharing of His afflictions (Col.
1:24); and he had the scars to prove it.[14]

C. Benediction (6:18)

VERSE 18. Paul has now come to the end of his epistle. He has
confronted the issue that had rocked the churches of Galatia, and
has set forth the truth which is inherent in the gospel—that men
are made truly free by God's grace alone, and this is received by
faith without the performance of any works of law. In his final
words, therefore, he prays that "the grace of our Lord Jesus
Christ" may be a precious reality in their spiritual con-
sciousness. Each of Paul's epistles closes with the mention of
this "grace," from the simplest reference "Grace be with you"
(Col. 4:18; I Tim. 6:21; II Tim. 4:22) to the most elaborate benediction, "The grace of the Lord Jesus Christ, and the love of God,
and the fellowship of the Holy Spirit, be with you all" (II Cor.
13:14). Only three of them, however, have the phrase "with your

---

[12]Otto Betz, "Stigma," TDNT, 7, 658-59.

[13]Josephus, The Jewish War 1, 197 (1. 10. 1).

[14]There is, of course, no Biblical evidence whatever to support the notion that
these "stigmata" were a supernatural reproducing in Paul's body of Christ's
nail prints. W. M. Ramsay has written, "The idea that these were marks similar
to those inflicted on the Saviour's body at the Crucifixion belongs to the 'Dark
Ages' of scholarship." A Historical Commentary on St. Paul's Epistle to the
Galatians (Grand Rapids, reprint ed., 1965), p. 472.

spirit" (Galatians, Philippians, Philemon). Perhaps Paul wished to emphasize the spiritual nature of true worship, in view of the faulty Galatian emphasis on ceremonies, although the occurrence of the same phrase in two other epistles makes this uncertain.

Of special interest is the inclusion of the word "brethren" as the last word in Paul's sentence. This is the only one of Paul's concluding benedictions which employs this term. Perhaps this was Paul's way of quietly reminding the Galatians that the severe language he had employed at times in the letter ("foolish Galatians," 3:1) did not mean he had cast them off. Much to the contrary, he regarded them as true Christian brothers, and fully expected them to deal properly with the false doctrine in their midst. They too had been set free from legalistic bondage and were full brothers with Paul. Together they were sharers of the freedom of God's sons.

Questions for Discussion

1. What impression do you think Paul's "large letters" made on his first readers?
2. Why would adoption of Jewish legalism enable Christians to avoid persecution?
3. In what ways were the Judaizers not keeping the very law they were promoting?
4. Can you suggest ways Christians can demonstrate that they glory in the cross of Christ?
5. How does Christ's cross crucify the world to the believer?
6. Who is meant by "the Israel of God"?
7. What were "the marks of the Lord Jesus" which Paul bore in his body?

Bibliography

Anstey, Martin. *The Romance of Bible Chronology*. London: Marshall Brothers, 1913.

Arndt, W. F., and Gingrich, F. W. *A Greek-English Lexicon of the New Testament*. Chicago: University of Chicago Press, 1957.

Barclay, William. *Flesh and Spirit*. Nashville: Abingdon Press, 1962.

———. *A New Testament Wordbook*. New York: Harper & Brothers, n. d.

Bruce, F. F. *The Book of the Acts*. In The New International Commentary series. Grand Rapids: Wm. B. Eerdmans Publishing Co., 1954.

———. "Galatian Problems. 1. Autobiographical Data." *Bulletin of the John Rylands Library*, vol. 51, no. 2 (Spring 1969).

———. "Galatian Problems. 2. North or South Galatians?" *Bulletin of the John Rylands Library, vol. 52, no. 2 (Spring 1970)*.

———. "Galatian Problems. 3. "The 'Other Gospel.' " *Bulletin of the John Rylands Library*, vol. 53, no. 2 (Spring 1971).

———. "Galatian Problems. 5. Galatians and Christian Origins." *Bulletin of the John Rylands University Library of Manchester*, vol. 55, no. 2 (Spring 1973).

Burton, Ernest DeWitt. *The Epistle to the Galatians*. In The International Critical Commentary series. Reprint. Edinburgh: T. & T. Clark, 1971.

Cole, R. A. *The Epistle of Paul to the Galatians*. In The Tyndale

Commentary series. Grand Rapids: Wm. B. Eerdmans Publishing Co., 1965.

Dana, H. C., and Mantey, J. R. *A Manual Grammar of the Greek New Testament.* New York: The Macmillan Co., 1946.

Davis, W. S. *A Day in Old Rome.* New York: Biblo and Tannen, 1972.

Deissman, Adolf. *Light from the Ancient East.* Reprint. Grand Rapids: Baker Book House, 1965.

Dio's Roman History, vol. 6. Translated by Ernest Cary in The Loeb Classical Library. New York: G. P. Putnam's Sons, 1917.

Eusebius Pamphili. *Ecclesiastical History.* Translated by Roy J. Deferrari in *The Fathers of the Church.* 1953. Reprint. Washington, D.C.: The Catholic University of America Press, 1969.

The Greek New Testament, ed. Kurt Aland et al. London: United Bible Societies, 1966.

Guthrie, Donald. *New Testament Introduction: The Pauline Epistles.* Chicago: Inter-Varsity Press, 1961.

Hamilton, Floyd E. *The Epistle to the Galatians.* In the Shield Bible Study series. Grand Rapids: Baker Book House, 1959.

Harrison, E. F. "The Epistle to the Galatians." In *Wycliffe Bible Commentary.* Chicago: Moody Press, 1962.

Hendriksen, William. *Exposition of Galatians.* In the New Testament Commentary series. Grand Rapids: Baker Book House, 1968.

Hoehner, Harold W. "The Duration of the Egyptian Bondage." *Bibliotheca Sacra* 126:504 (October 1969).

The Interpreter's Dictionary of the Bible, ed. George Arthur Buttrick. New York: Abingdon Press, 1962.

Jewett, Robert. "The Agitators and the Galatian Congregation." *New Testament Studies* 17:2 (January 1971).

Josephus. *The Jewish War*. Translated by H. St. J. Thackeray, in The Loeb Classical Library. Cambridge: Harvard University Press, 1956.

Kent, Homer A., Jr. *Jerusalem to Rome*. Grand Rapids: Baker Book House and BMH Books, 1972.

Kenyon, Frederic G. *Handbook to the Textual Criticism of the New Testament*. Reprint, Grand Rapids: Wm. B. Eerdmans Publishing Co., 1953.

Kittel, Gerhard, and Friedrich, Gerhard, eds. *Theological Dictionary of the New Testament*. Translated by Geoffrey W. Bromiley. Grand Rapids: Wm. B. Eerdmans Publishing Co., 1964-1972.

Klassen, William. "Galatians 6:17." *The Expository Times* 81:12 (September 1970).

Lenski, R. C. H. *The Interpretation of St. Paul's Epistle to the Galatians, to the Ephesians, and to the Philippians*. Columbus: The Wartburg Press, 1946.

Lightfoot, J. B. *The Epistle of St. Paul to the Galatians*. Reprint. Grand Rapids: Zondervan Publishing House, n.d.

Luther, Martin. *A Commentary on St. Paul's Epistle to the Galatians*. Translated by Theodore Graebner. Grand Rapids: Zondervan Publishing House, n.d.

Lyall, Francis. "Roman Law in the Writings of Paul— Adoption." *Journal of Biblical Literature*, vol. 88, part 4 (December 1969).

Meyer, H. A. W. *Critical and Exegetical Handbook to the Epistle to the Galatians*. New York: Funk & Wagnalls, 1884.

The New Bible Dictionary, ed. J. D. Douglas. Grand Rapids: Wm. B. Eerdmans Publishing Co., 1962.

Parker, Pierson. "Once More, Acts and Galatians." *Journal of Biblical Literature*, vol. 86, part 2 (June 1967).

Ramsay, W. M. *The Church in the Roman Empire*. Reprint. Grand Rapids: Baker Book House, 1954.

_____. *The Cities of St. Paul*. Reprint. Grand Rapids: Baker Book House, 1949.

_____. *A Historical Commentary on St. Paul's Epistle to the Galatians*. Reprint. Grand Rapids: Baker Book House, 1965.

_____. *St. Paul the Traveller and Roman Citizen*. Reprint. Grand Rapids: Baker Book House, 1949.

Rendall, Frederic. "The Epistle to the Galatians." In *The Expositor's Greek Testament*. Grand Rapids: Wm. B. Eerdmans Publishing Co., n.d.

Ridderbos, Herman N. *The Epistle of Paul to the Churches of Galatia*. In The New International Commentary series. Grand Rapids: Wm. B. Eerdmans Publishing Co., 1956.

Riggs, Jack R. "The Length of Israel's Sojourn in Egypt." *Grace Journal*, vol. 12, no. 1 (Winter 1971).

Roberts, Alexander, and Donaldson, James, eds. *Ante-Nicene Fathers*. Reprint. Grand Rapids: Wm. B. Eerdmans Publishing Co., 1951.

Robertson, A. T. *A Grammar of the Greek New Testament in the Light of Historical Research*. Nashville: Broadman Press, 1934.

Ropes, James Hardy. *The Singular Problem of the Epistle to the Galatians*. Harvard Theological Studies 14. Cambridge: Harvard University Press, 1929.

Ross, Alexander. "The Epistle to the Galatians." In *The New Bible Commentary*, ed. F. Davidson. Grand Rapids: Wm. B. Eerdmans Publishing Co., 1954.

Scofield, C. I., ed. *Scofield Reference Bible*. Rev. ed. New York: Oxford University Press, 1967.

Speiser, E. A. *Genesis*. In The Anchor Bible series. Garden City: Doubleday and Co., 1964.

Tenney, Merrill C. *Galatians: The Charter of Christian Liberty*. Grand Rapids: Wm. B. Eerdmans Publishing Co., 1957.

Vincent, Marvin R. *Word Studies in the New Testament*. Reprint. Grand Rapids: Wm. B. Eerdmans Publishing Co., 1946.

Vos, Howard F. *Galatians—A Call to Christian Liberty*. In Everyman's Bible Commentary series. Chicago: Moody Press, 1971.

Wright, George Ernest. *Biblical Archaeology*. Philadelphia: Westminster Press, 1962.

Wuest, Kenneth S. *Galatians in the Greek New Testament*. Grand Rapids: Wm. B. Eerdmans Publishing Co., 1944.